Study Guide
and Workbook for

Essentials of Financial Management

Text and Cases

Study Guide and Workbook for Essentials of Financial Management

Text and Cases

George C. Philippatos
The Pennsylvania State University
Donald A. Nast
The Florida State University

Holden-Day, Inc.
San Francisco

Düsseldorf Johannesburg London Mexico Panama
São Paulo Singapore Sydney Toronto

STUDY GUIDE AND WORKBOOK FOR
ESSENTIALS OF FINANCIAL MANAGEMENT: TEXT AND CASES

500 Sansome Street, San Francisco, CA 94111

Printed in the United States of America

ISBN: 0-8162-6696-4

1 2 3 4 5 6 7 8 9 0 LC 8 0 7 9 8 7 6 5 4

Preface

The *Study Guide and Workbook* for *Essentials of Financial Management: Text and Cases* is designed for use by students of introductory courses in financial management. The basic pedagogic purpose of the *Study Guide and Workbook* is threefold: (1) To delineate the central theme and outline the highlights of each chapter in *Essentials of Financial Management: Text and Cases.* This is achieved in the first section of each chapter of the study guide, which states the theme in broad strokes and proceeds with a detailed outline of the salient issues in the chapter. (2) To enable the students to test their newly acquired knowledge on the basic concepts and decision-making situations of modern financial management. This is attained by answering the Questions for Self-Examination and verifying the test results by reference to the Answers section at the end of the book. (3) To enable the students to practice and test their knowledge of the basic methodology and techniques employed in the quest for solutions to financial problems. This is achieved by the utilization of the sections on Problems for Practice and Problems for Self-Examination. Here again, the students can validate their solutions by reference to the Answers section.

Our experience with students who utilize study guides, workbooks, and other learning aids for knowledge and scoring performance in examinations leads us to suggest the following successful sequence of study: (1) The students should become familiar with the central theme and detailed outline of each chapter. (2) They then should proceed to study the chapter in detail and make mental notes about various concepts and techniques. (3) When the material is well in perspective, the students should test their conceptual understanding by answering the Questions for Self-Examination and studying the Problems for Practice. (4) Finally, they should test their logical understanding by solving the Problems for Self-Examination. We believe that the above sequence, with some minor variations to accommodate individual study habits, can be useful to all students in introductory courses in financial management.

A number of respected colleagues have provided valuable inputs to the material. Special thanks are due to Jeffrey D. Parkhurst, The Pennsylvania State University, and Michael A. Fettig, The Florida State University, for their serious collaboration and contributions to the book. We would also like to express our appreciation to Helen Spicher, Ruth Ann Nast, Anna Margaret Peters, and Beth A. Wheland for their cheerful typing and proofing of the many versions of the manuscript. Finally, our families have, as always, contributed their fair share of encouragement, support, and patience. Only a special note of thanks can express our deep appreciation for their extraordinary contribution.

George C. Philippatos,
University Park, Pennsylvania

Donald A. Nast,
Tallahassee, Florida

Contents

Study Guide
and Workbook for

Essentials of Financial Management

Text and Cases

1 Introduction to Some Fundamental Concepts

Theme Chapter 1 briefly presents a few concepts of the firm and then traces the evolution of financial management.

I Financial management is concerned with the acquisition and financing of long- and short-term assets and the effects of the inflow and outflow of funds upon managerial objectives.

A The traditional goal of profit maximization may no longer be operationally meaningful.

1 It provides ambiguous and limited choices among alternative courses of action.
2 It overlooks the qualitative benefits associated with the various courses of action.
3 It overlooks the behavioral dynamics of current organizations.

B The structure of the business enterprise has changed.

1 There has been a general separation of the ownership of the firm from those who manage it.
2 Goals other than profit maximization may motivate management. A few alternatives could be
(a) Survival
(b) Sales maximization
(c) Personal gratification

II The various concepts of the firm may be classified as either holistic or behavioral.

A Holistic concepts are those that view the firm as a single entity with homogeneous behavior.

1 They emphasize collective rather than individual action.
2 They assume predetermined patterns of rational behavior.
3 They posit a lucid goal orientation for the firm.
4 They assume that action is a response to the external environment (market).

B Behavioral concepts are those that view the actions of the firm as a stream of interrelated activities.

1 They assume it is individuals within an organization that act.
2 Individual behavior is viewed as being conditioned by one's personality as well as one's environment.
3 Managerial goals are usually complex.

III Valuation is the central theme of financial management.

A Consumer demand results in a derived demand for investment; this derived demand results in a derived demand for funds to finance the investment.

B For publicly held corporations, these interrelated activities are stored and evaluated in the securities market.

IV Financial management has evolved as an outgrowth of economics.

A Its origin as a discipline coincided with the emergence of national markets and the merger movement at the turn of this century.

1 The creation of corporate giants also created enormous budgeting and financing complications.
2 The major issues of financial management at this point in time were
(a) The size and composition of the firm's assets and liabilities
(b) The optimal mix of debt and equity
(c) Dividend policy
(d) Market valuation of the firm's securities

B During the 1920s the economy underwent the birth of new industries, the emergence of national advertising, and the improvement of distribution practices.

1 Firms experienced high profit margins.
2 The impact upon financial management was manifested by improved methods of planning and control, concern with liquidity, and a greater interest in financial structure.

C The severe economic depression of the 1930s resulted in business reorganization. Attention in the discipline concentrated on liquidity, solvency, and financial structure.

D The next changes occurred in the early 1950s.

1 Managerial emphasis shifted from profitability analysis to cash-flow generation.
2 Financial management developed an interest in internal management procedures and controls.
3 A change in outlook occurred from that of the outside analyst to the role of the inside manager.

E Financial management during the late 1950s and early 1960s was characterized by a series of debates on the cost of capital, optimal capital structure, and the effects of capital structure on the cost of capital and the market valuation of the firm.

F A renewed interest in liquidity and profit margins, and new thoughts on the efficiency of trading rules and portfolio selection criteria, have characterized the discipline from the mid-1960s to the present.

QUESTIONS FOR SELF-EXAMINATION

True or False

____ 1 Holistic concepts of the firm are those that emphasize the unity of the firm and its behavior.

____ 2 One of the recurring concerns of financial management is liquidity.

____ 3 Profit maximization tends to be a holistic concept of the firm, whereas personal gratification tends to be more of a behavioral concept of the firm.

____ 4 Investment demand is the central theme of financial management.

____ 5 The managers of a firm necessarily have the same business objectives as the owners of the firm.

2 The Financial Management Program

Theme Chapter 2 outlines the financial management program and introduces the concept of capital budgeting.

I The goal of modern financial management is to maximize the firm's market value by optimally matching the sources and uses of corporate funds.

A There are three basic concerns in financial management:

1 What specific assets should the firm purchase?
2 What is the total volume of funds that the firm should commit?
3 How should the firm acquire the funds necessary to implement its investment decisions?

B Investment-project evaluation deals with two criteria:

1 Managerial preferences that are invariably expressed by a utility function.
2 Managerial expectations about the future benefits and costs of an investment.

C Since the future is uncertain, managerial expectations are often expressed by a probability distribution of expected returns.

1 The measure of central tendency is often the mean of the above distribution.
2 The measure of dispersion is often the standard deviation of the above distribution.
(a) The standard deviation is used as a proxy for the business risk of a project.
(b) Business risk is the variability of future returns about the average expected return.

D One should select a portfolio (combination) of projects that protects the firm from massive failures — portfolio risk.

1 Consider the effects of each project upon the other assets of the firm — the covariability of project returns.
2 Diversify one's investments to minimize portfolio risk.

E Financial risk refers to the relative inability of the firm to meet the claims of its creditors.

F Joel Dean has proposed a 10-step investment program:

1 Search for profitable investment opportunities.
2 Verify each project to be congruent with the firm's long-range plans.
3 List each verified project on the short-range capital budget.
4 Calculate a summary measure of each project's worth.
5 Compare the proposals, and select the one(s) consistent with the firm's selection criteria.
6 Control the authorized outlays of the project(s).
7 Evaluate the realized outcomes of the project(s) with the expected outcomes.
8 Retire the project(s).

9 Prepare the pertinent project reports.
10 Estimate the rate of return for the project(s).

II Investment is motivated by four considerations:

A Replacement, which involves expenditures for the replacement of worn-out or obsolete assets.

B Expansion, which involves capital-widening decisions to accommodate the firm's dynamic growth.

C Modernization, which involves capital-deepening decisions to facilitate the cost-reducing efforts of the firm.

D Strategic investment, which involves capital-budgeting decisions whose monetary returns are not immediate or even measurable.

III Capital budgeting is concerned with the allocation of the firm's financial resources among the available opportunities congruent with the goals of the firm.

A The pool of funds, a general record of the money flowing through the firm, has two components:

1 Sources of funds include transactions that increase liabilities or capital or activities which reduce assets.
2 Uses of funds include transactions that reduce liabilities or capital or activities which increase assets.

B Cash flow is the receipt or payment of an amount of money.

1 Gross cash flow is the sum of profits after taxes plus accounting depreciation charges.
2 Net cash flow is the sum of profits after taxes.

C The investment decision concerns itself with the two basic principles of the rational investor:

1 He prefers larger returns to smaller returns, everything else held constant.
2 He prefers early returns to more distant returns, everything else held constant.

IV Although they suffer from severe shortcomings, the widespread use of some simple capital-budgeting techniques warrants their consideration.

A The urgency criterion is used to justify the acceptance of capital projects on the basis of emergency, necessity, or timeliness.

1 However, this criterion lacks objectivity and generality.
2 Furthermore, the urgency criterion fails to measure the capital productivity of a project and its overall earnings effect on the firm.

B The payback-period criterion implies the adoption of an investment project if it pays for itself plus some acceptable profit margin, within a specific time period.

1 Payback period = initial cost/annual cash flow or
Payback period = (initial cost plus profit)/annual cash flow

2 The payback-period criterion has these advantages:
(a) It is easy to use.
(b) It is used only for screening proposals.
(c) It is a useful approximation of the value of risky investments whose rate of capital usage is hard to predict.
3 The payback-period criterion has these disadvantages:
(a) The generality of the technique is constrained.
(b) It overplays the importance of liquidity.

(c) It ignores capital usage and economic life.
(d) It fails to consider returns after the payback period.
(e) It overstates the worth of flows within the payback period.
(f) It violates the two basic principles of the rational investor.

C The plowback criterion restricts investments to the amount of funds generated internally by the firm.

1 It is an easy criterion to use.
2 However, the firm will forego many profitable investment opportunities by using it.

V Other approximate measures of investment performance.

A There are three commonly used versions of accounting rates of return:

1 Original book method: Divide the average annual net income by the original book value (cost) of the asset.

Rate of return = average annual net income/original cost

2 Average book method: This method accounts for capital usage.

Rate of return = average annual net income/(original cost-salvage value)/2

3 Year-by-year book method: Using the original book method, calculate the rate of return for each year.

B Accounting rates of return have the advantages of ease and simplicity.

C However, they violate the second principle of the rational investor by overlooking the uncertainty of later cash flows. Furthermore, they give biased and inconsistent rankings.

VI Another ex post measure of investment performance is return on investment (ROI).

A Return on investment equals the profit margin times the turnover ratio or the ratio of profits to assets.

ROI = profits/sales × sales/assets or

ROI = profits/assets

B The profit margin measures the relative efficiency with which the firm produces its output.

C The turnover ratio measures the relative efficiency in the utilization of the firm's plant and equipment.

D Two additional ex post measures of return are

1 Return on equity (ROE)

ROE = profits/net worth

2 Return on capital (ROC)

ROC = profits/(liabilities and net worth)

VII Two other approximate methods of investment performance are also presented:

A Hoskold's method, which divides the difference between the cash-flow charges and sinking fund deposit by the initial investment cost.

1 This method requires that uniform annual deposits be made into a sinking fund earning a specified rate of return.
2 At the end of the asset's useful life, the value of the sinking fund should be equal to the amount required for replacing the asset.

B Undiscounted benefit-cost ratio, which is a ratio of the total benefits and costs of a project without any discount for futurity or risk.

1 The undiscounted gross benefit-cost ratio is the summation of all the cash flows generated from a project (B) divided by the original cost of the project (C).

$$\text{Ratio} = \sum_{t=1}^{n} B_t/C$$

2 The undiscounted net benefit-cost ratio is the summation of the difference between all the cash flows generated from a project and the accounting depreciation charges ($B_t - D_t$) divided by the original cost of the project (C).

$$\text{Ratio} = \sum_{t=1}^{n} (B_t - D_t)/C \text{ or}$$

$$\text{Ratio} = \sum_{t=1}^{n} B_t/C - 1$$

since $C = \sum_{t=1}^{n} D_t$ for a nominal, final salvage value.

QUESTIONS FOR SELF-EXAMINATION

True or False

____ 1 Investment-project evaluation concerns managerial preferences and managerial expectations.

____ 2 Through diversification one hopes to maximize his return.

____ 3 Sources of funds include transactions that decrease liabilities or capital.

____ 4 Gross and net cash flows are two measures of income streams.

____ 5 The urgency criterion argues that certain projects are essential to the survival of the firm and, therefore, should be objectively scrutinized.

____ 6 The accounting rates of return have the advantage of accounting for uncertainty in the flows of investments.

____ 7 Capital-widening decisions refer to expenditures that will facilitate the cost-reducing efforts of the firm.

____ 8 Dean's 10-step investment program begins with a search for profitable investment opportunities.

____ 9 The covariability of project returns refers to the effects of each project upon the other assets of the firm.

____ 10 The average book method for approximating investment performance accounts for capital usage.

____ 11 Portfolio risk refers to the relative inability of the firm to meet the claims of its creditors.

Multiple Choice

____ 1 Which of the following is not one of the three basic investment concerns?
- (a) What assets should the firm purchase?
- (b) How should the firm acquire the necessary funds?
- (c) How does the firm reduce its tax liability?
- (d) What is the total volume of funds that the firm should commit?

____ 2 The payback criterion implies the adoption of an investment proposal if the
- (a) project is necessary to the livelihood of the firm.
- (b) value of the project's sinking fund is equal to the replacement cost.
- (c) firm prefers early returns to more distant returns.
- (d) project pays for itself within a specific time period.

_____ 3 _____ risk is the variability of future returns about the average expected return from a single investment project.

(a) Business
(b) Portfolio
(c) Market
(d) Financial

_____ 4 Which of the following is not a motivation for investment?

(a) Modernization
(b) Strategic investment
(c) Expansion
(d) Plowback

_____ 5 Which of the following is not a disadvantage of the payback period criterion?

(a) Its generality is constrained.
(b) It is used only for screening proposals.
(c) It overplays the importance of liquidity.
(d) It may fail to consider some returns.

PROBLEMS FOR PRACTICE

1 The investment policy of Leer Company is to accept investment projects only if the payback period is four years or less. Project A has an initial cost of $16,000 and is expected to yield $4,500 per year for the next five years. Project B has an expected yield of $6,000 per year for seven years, and its initial cost is $26,000. Is either project acceptable?

Solution

Project A:

$$\text{Payback period} = \frac{\$16{,}000}{\$\ 4{,}500} = 3.55 \text{ years}$$

Project B:

$$\text{Payback period} = \frac{\$26{,}000}{\$\ 6{,}000} = 4.33 \text{ years}$$

Accept Project A and reject Project B.

2 Leer Company wishes to compare the rate of return of Project A and Project B using the original book method. Calculate the rate of return for each project whose salvage value at the end of its useful life is nominal. Use straight-line depreciation.

Solution

Per Year		*Project A*		*Project B*
Cash Flow		$4,500		$6,000
Depreciation	($16,000/5) =	3,200	($26,000/7) =	3,714
Net income		$1,300		$2,286
Rate of return	($1,300/$16,000) =	8.13%	($2,286/$26,000) =	8.79%

3 Determine the undiscounted gross benefit-cost ratio for the above projects A and B.

Solution

Project A: $\sum_{t=1}^{5} B_t = \$22{,}500$ Ratio $= \dfrac{\$22{,}500}{\$16{,}000} = 1.41$

Project B: $\sum_{t=1}^{7} B_t = \$42{,}000$ Ratio $= \dfrac{\$42{,}000}{\$26{,}000} = 1.62$

Note: The ranking of Projects A and B by the payback period is reversed by the rate of return (original book method) and the undiscounted gross benefit-cost ratio.

PROBLEMS FOR SELF-EXAMINATION

4 Projects C and D have the following estimated annual cash flows:

Year(s)	*Project C*	*Project D*
1	$ 0	$ 5,000
2–4	12,000	10,000
5	12,000	5,000

The initial costs for Projects C and D are $40,000 and $30,000, respectively. What is the payback period for each project?

Solution

Project C: Total amount paid back by end of fourth year = $

Amount remaining to be paid back during fifth year = $40,000 − $ = $

$ /$12,000 = years to pay back remainder

Payback period = 4 + = years

Project D: Total amount paid back by end of third year = $

Amount remaining = $30,000 − $ = $

$ /$10,000 = years

Payback period = 3 + = years

5 For the above Projects C and D, calculate the undiscounted gross benefit-cost ratios.

Solution

Project C: $\sum_{t=1}^{5} B_t =$ $ Ratio $= \frac{\$}{\$40{,}000} =$

Project D: $\sum_{t=1}^{5} B_t =$ $ Ratio $= \frac{\$}{\$30{,}000} =$

6 Two investment projects, E and F, are being analyzed by the financial manager of Tier Company. Project E costs $75,000, and Project F costs $90,000. The data reveal the following estimated cash flows:

Year	*Project E*	*Project F*
1	$10,000	$40,000
2	20,000	30,000
3	25,000	20,000
4	30,000	20,000
5	30,000	20,000
6	30,000	20,000

Tier Company employs the payback period as an investment criterion. Determine the payback period for each project.

Solution 9

Project E:

Project F:

7 For additional analysis, the financial manager of Tier Company also considers the undiscounted gross benefit-cost ratio. Calculate this ratio for Projects E and F.

Solution

Project E:

Project F:

3 Analysis of Financial Statements and the Flow of Funds

Theme Analysis of the historical information contained in the financial statements of a firm enables management to evaluate past performance and form tentative expectations about future trends.

I There are four basic financial statements:

A Income statement

B Balance sheet

C Statement of retained earnings

D Statement of sources and uses of funds

II The income statement, or profit and loss statement, details the firm's sales revenue along with the operating and administrative expenses for a given time period.

A This statement represents the summation of changes (flows) in various classifications.

B An insider can use income statement figures to compute performance variances.

III The balance sheet deals with the financial position of the firm at a given moment in time.

A This statement shows the values of three basic classifications:

Assets = liabilities + net worth

B Income statement and balance-sheet figures are used to compute the realized rate of return on invested assets (ROI), equity (ROE), and total capital (ROC).

IV The statement of retained earnings complements the income statement by reflecting all changes in the owners' equity and provides a link between consecutive balance sheets via the owners' equity account.

V The statement of sources and uses of funds is a flow statement that shows the increases or decreases in net working capital and cash over a given time period.

A The changes in the individual accounts delineate the net flows of funds resulting from management actions and/or prevailing economic conditions.

B Sources of funds are transactions that increase liabilities or net worth or transactions which reduce asset values.

C Uses of funds are transactions that reduce liabilities or net worth or transactions which increase asset values.

VI Cash-flow analysis is used to measure the firm's ability to generate funds.

A The elements of cash flow are streams of receipts and disbursements properly discounted for futurity and uncertainty.

1 Gross cash flow is defined as profit after taxes plus accounting depreciation.
2 Net cash flow is defined as profit after taxes.

B Income flow refers to revenues and expenditures.

C There are three possible time sequences between cash flows and income flows:

1 Leading
2 Coincident
3 Lagging

VII There are three types of depreciation:

A Physical depreciation is the normal wear and tear on an asset that reduces its productivity.

B Accounting depreciation refers to the reported charges as per the bookkeeping practices of the corporation.

C Economic depreciation is the rate of decrease in the revenues generated by an asset because of the gradual obsolescence of the asset or the diminishing demand for its output.

VIII There are three major methods of computing accounting depreciation:

A Straight-line depreciation writes off the cost of an asset, C, equally over N years. The sum of the depreciation charges, D, equals the difference between the asset's cost and its salvage value S.

1 Depreciation for the ith and every year:

$$D_i = (C - S)/N$$

2 Total depreciation charges:

$$\sum_{i=1}^{n} D_i = C - S$$

B The double-declining balance method of depreciation charges a rate on the undepreciated balance of an asset which is twice that of straight-line depreciation.

1 Depreciation for the ith year:

$$D_i = 2/N\,[C(1 - 2/N)^{i-1}]$$

2 Undepreciated balance at the end of the ith year:

$$\text{Balance} = C(1 - 2/N)^i$$

3 IRS rules permit a firm to switch to the straight-line method before the end of the ith year.

C The sum-of-the-years'-digits method of depreciation deducts a declining fraction from the original cost of the asset. Depreciation for the ith year is

$$D_i = (N - i + 1)C/1/2\,[N(N + 1)] \qquad \text{where } N > i > 1$$

IX The tax shield effect is the proportionate decrease in the amount of corporate taxes paid as a consequence of depreciation charges decreasing the amount of taxable earnings.

A The straight-line method of depreciation has the least advantageous tax shield.

B The other two methods of depreciation are accelerated techniques and vie as the best choice according to the patterns of inflows.

C The tax aspects of depreciation involve

1 The tax savings on the discounted value of depreciation.
2 The discounted value of the expected earnings after taxes.

QUESTIONS FOR SELF-EXAMINATION

True or False

_____ 1 The balance sheet represents the summation of flows in various classifications.

_____ 2 The statement of sources and uses of funds shows the changes in the net working capital and cash over a given time period.

_____ 3 Cash-flow analysis is used as a record of the money flowing in and out of the firm.

_____ 4 Economic depreciation refers to the reported charges as per the bookkeeping practices of the firm.

_____ 5 Straight-line depreciation is the only method that has equal depreciation charges for every year in the life of an asset.

_____ 6 The tax shield effect is the proportionate decrease in the amount of corporate taxes paid as a consequence of depreciation charges decreasing the market value of an asset.

_____ 7 Net cash flow equals gross cash flow minus accounting depreciation.

_____ 8 Once a firm has begun to depreciate an asset with a specific method, it must always continue to use that method on the asset.

_____ 9 The elements of cash flow need not be discounted for futurity or uncertainty because one is only interested in the general direction of flow and not its magnitude.

_____ 10 Transactions that increase asset values are classified as uses of funds.

Multiple Choice

_____ 1 Which of the following is not a flow statement?
(a) Statement of sources and uses of funds
(b) Profit and loss statement
(c) Statement of retained earnings
(d) Balance sheet

_____ 2 The statement of retained earnings provides a link between consecutive balance sheets via the ________ account.
(a) working capital
(b) owner's equity
(c) current assets
(d) finished goods

_____ 3 The double-declining balance method and the sum-of-the-years'-digits method of depreciation each have a more advantageous tax shield than the straight-line method because
(a) they are harder or more difficult to use.
(b) the IRS wants to discourage the use of the straight-line method.
(c) they consider economic depreciation and the straight-line method does not.
(d) they depreciate a larger percentage of the asset early in its economic life.

_____ 4 An insider can use the ________ to compute performance variances.
(a) statement of sources and uses of funds
(b) balance sheet
(c) statement of earned surplus
(d) income statement

_____ 5 The elements of cash flow are ________ properly discounted for futurity and uncertainty.

(a) revenues and expenditures
(b) deposits and withdrawals
(c) receipts and disbursements
(d) accounts receivable and accounts payable

PROBLEMS FOR PRACTICE

1 Following are two balance sheets for Sheer Company. Construct the statement of sources and uses of funds.

Sheer Company, December 31, 1972 and 1973, ($000)

	1973	*1972*
Assets		
Cash	$ 25	$ 22
Accounts receivable	26	30
Inventories	11	9
Fixed assets (net)	50	46
	$112	$107
Liabilities and Net Worth		
Accounts payable	$ 17	$ 16
Bank loan	21	21
Long-term bonds	18	19
Common stock	56	51
	$112	$107

Solution

Sheer Company sources and uses of funds (1972–1973)

Sources of Funds	
Decrease in accounts receivable	$ 4
Increase in accounts payable	1
Increase in common stock	5
Total sources	$10
Uses of Funds	
Increase in cash	$ 3
Increase in inventories	2
Increase in fixed assets	4
Decrease in long-term bonds	1
Total uses	$10

2 Sheer Company has purchased a new stamping machine for $40,000. Its expected life is four years with no remaining salvage value. Compare the depreciation expense by the (a) straight line, (b) sum-of-the-years' digits, and (c) double-declining balance methods. Convert the double-declining balance to straight line in the fourth year.

Solution

(a) Straight line:

$$\frac{\$40{,}000}{4 \text{ years}} = \$10{,}000/\text{year}$$

(b) Sum-of-the-years' digits:

$1 + 2 + 3 + 4 = 10$

Fractions for the years are $\frac{4}{10}, \frac{3}{10}, \frac{2}{10}, \frac{1}{10}$.

(c) Double-declining balance:

Year 1 $\frac{\$40{,}000}{4 \text{ years}} \times 2 = \$10{,}000 \times 2 = \$20{,}000$

Year 2 $\frac{\$40{,}000 - \$20{,}000}{4} \times 2 = \$5{,}000 \times 2 = \$10{,}000$

Year 3 $\frac{\$20{,}000 - \$10{,}000}{4} \times 2 = \$2{,}500 \times 2 = \$5{,}000$

Year 4 $\$10{,}000 - \$5{,}000 = \$5{,}000$

Year	*Straight Line*	*Sum-of-the-Years' Digits*	*Double-Declining Balance*
1	$10,000	$16,000	$20,000
2	10,000	12,000	10,000
3	10,000	8,000	5,000
4	10,000	4,000	5,000
	$40,000	$40,000	$40,000

PROBLEMS FOR SELF-EXAMINATION

3 It is estimated that a new machine costing $60,000 will yield an annual cash flow before taxes of $20,000 for the next five years. Sum-of-the-years' digits method of depreciation is employed. Assume no salvage value and a 50% tax rate. Calculate the gross cash flows for each year.

Solution

Sum of the years =

Year	*Cash Flow before Taxes*	*Cash Flow after Taxes*	*Depreciation*	*Gross Cash Flow*
1	$20,000	$	$20,000	$ 30,000
2	20,000			
3	20,000			
4	20,000			
5	20,000			
			$60,000	$110,000

4 Construct the statement of sources and uses of funds from the successive balance sheets of Pauly & Sons.

Pauly & Sons, June 30, 1973 and 1974 ($000)

	1973	*1974*
Assets		
Cash	$ 62	$ 65
Accounts receivable	49	50
Inventories	38	36
Gross plant and equipment	123	123
Accumulated depreciation	21	16
Net plant and equipment	102	107
	$251	$258
Liabilities and Net Worth		
Accounts payable	$ 45	$ 49
Bank loan	26	24
Preferred stock	20	20
Common stock	160	165
	$251	$258

Solution

Pauly & Sons, sources and uses of funds (1973–1974)

Sources of Funds	
Decrease in	$
Decrease in	
Decrease in	
Increase in	
Total sources	$
Uses of Funds	
Increase in	$
Decrease in	
Decrease in	
	$

5 A new packaging machine costs $48,000 and has an expected life of six years with no salvage value. With a 50% tax rate, compare the gross cash flows for each year resulting from the straight-line and double-declining balance methods of depreciation. Convert the double-declining balance to straight-line depreciation for the last two years. Following are the estimated cash flows before taxes:

Year	*Cash Flow before Taxes*
1	$18,000
2	16,000
3	14,000
4	12,000
5	12,000
6	12,000

Solution

6 Calculate the depreciation during the third year for an asset costing $120,000. It is expected to have a 10-year life with no salvage value. Determine the depreciation by the (a) straight-line, (b) sum-of-the-years' digits, and (c) double-declining balance methods.

Solution

(a) Straight line:

(b) Sum-of-the-years' digits:

(c) Double-declining balance:

4 Capital-Budgeting Techniques: The Case of Certainty

Theme The net-present-value, internal rate of discount, and discounted benefit-cost ratio methods of ranking and selecting capital-budgeting proposals are more sophisticated than previously mentioned methods and are also considered exact. Although they do not account for the uncertainty of expected returns, these techniques are compatible with both principles of the rational investor.

I Expected returns are discounted because of futurity and uncertainty.

A Futurity refers to the time value of money.

1 Early returns are preferred to more distant returns.
2 For the proper reward, one is often willing to forego some present consumption for future benefits.

B Uncertainty is the lack of perfect foresight about future events.

1 The chance exists that streams of future returns may not materialize as expected.
2 Because uncertainty is elusive and nonmeasurable, one attempts to reduce it to risk.
3 Risk is measurable; specifically, one desires measures of business risk and financial risk.

II Present value is the current worth of an amount of money to be received in the future, properly discounted for futurity.

A Present value equals the discounted future or terminal value of an expected income (expenditure).

$$PV = R_n/(1 + r)^n$$

where PV = present value
R_n = terminal value
r = annual interest rate
n = number of years until R_n is received

B If the income stream is characterized by a variable return, then the formula becomes

$$PV = \sum_{n=1}^{t} R_n/(1 + r)^n$$

C If the income stream is a perpetuity, that is, a stream of equal, yearly payments forever, then the formula is

$$PV = R_i/r$$

where R_i = yearly payment expressed as an amount

D Present value is the converse of the compound growth concept.

E Two important considerations of the present value equation are

1 Present value is inversely related to the interest or discount rate.
2 It is assumed that the flows are reinvested at the rate of discount.

III Three capital-budgeting criteria that account for futurity are

A The net-present-value method, which uses the difference between the discounted cash inflows and the discounted cash outflows as a measure of the absolute profits from an investment.

$$\text{NPV} = \sum_{n=1}^{t} R_n/(1 + r)^n - \sum_{n=1}^{t} C_n/(1 + r)^n$$

where R_n = inflow for year n
C_n = outflow for year n
r = discount rate

1 Net present value uses the cost of capital as the discount rate.
2 Accept all projects within a given risk class that have a positive NPV. When considering mutually exclusive projects, accept the one with the largest positive NPV.

B The internal-rate-of-discount method, which expresses the estimated value of a project as a single overall rate of return per annum.

$$\sum_{n=1}^{t} R_n/(1+\rho)^n = \sum_{n=1}^{t} C_n/(1 + \rho)^n$$

where ρ = internal rate of discount

1 Note that the discount rate, r, used in the net-present-value method is the given cost of capital and different from the internal rate of discount, ρ, which is computed by trial and error.
2 The internal-rate-of-discount method can be employed in either of two modes:
(a) Conditional ρ maximization: Given a limited amount of investment funds, choose the combination of projects or the single incremental project that maximizes ρ.
(b) ρ-r comparison: When considering incremental investment proposals, adopt a project if the incremental ρ — a measure of expected profitability — exceeds r, the market rate of interest.

C The discounted gross benefit-cost ratio — also called the profitability index — which is the ratio of the present value of future benefits to the present value of the outlays.

$$\text{BCR} = \sum_{n=1}^{t} R_n(1 + r)^{-n} \Big/ \sum_{n=1}^{t} C_n(1 + r)^{-n}$$

where r = required rate of return

1 The net, discounted benefit-cost ratio is equal to the gross ratio minus 1.
2 If the profitability index of a proposal is greater than 1, then accept the project. If it is equal to 1, the project is expected to break even. If it is less than 1, then reject the project.
3 Although the NPV method and the BCR method give identical accept signals, the ranking of investment projects by these methods will generally be different.
(a) The NPV results are absolute magnitudes, whereas the BCR results are relative rankings.
(b) The BCR method is the more appropriate capital-rationing technique because one should be interested in the relative ranking of investment proposals.

IV Three other investment criteria are

A The net-terminal-value method, which compounds the cash inflows and outflows forward to some future, terminal date.

1 It is the converse of net present value.
2 Accept a project if the difference between the compounded benefits and costs is greater than zero.

B The annual gross benefit-cost ratio, which converts discounted annual costs into equivalent average annual returns.

1 The net ratio equals the gross ratio minus 1.
2 Accept a project if the gross ratio of annual benefits to annual costs is greater than 1.

C The net-costs criterion, which involves the minimization of the discounted average costs of the entire productive activity of the firm.

QUESTIONS FOR SELF-EXAMINATION

True or False

_____ 1 Futurity is the lack of perfect foresight about future events.

_____ 2 The present-value concept involves the equivalence and interchangeability of two sums of money at different points in time.

_____ 3 The discount rate used in the net-present-value method is the same as the discount rate used in the internal-rate-of-discount method.

_____ 4 The NPV method and the BCR method give identical investment project rankings but will generally give different accept signals.

_____ 5 Present value is inversely related to the discount rate.

_____ 6 Because uncertainty is elusive and nonmeasurable, one attempts to reduce it to a measure of profitability.

_____ 7 The present-value concept is to the net-present-value method as the compound-growth concept is to the net-terminal-value method.

_____ 8 When the gross, discounted benefit-cost ratio method is used as the capital-budgeting technique, one should accept a proposal if the profitability index is greater than unity.

_____ 9 The net-present value, internal-rate-of-discount, and discounted benefit-cost ratio methods all account for futurity and uncertainty.

Multiple Choice

_____ 1 The NPV results are absolute magnitudes, whereas the BCR_D results are _____

(a) compounded cash flows.
(b) equivalent average annual returns.
(c) a rate of return per annum.
(d) relative rankings.

_____ 2 The net-costs criterion involves the _____ of discounted average costs.

(a) equalization
(b) minimization
(c) maximization
(d) neutralization

_____ 3 The present-value concept assumes that the cash flows are _____

(a) inversely related to current worth.
(b) equal, yearly payments forever.
(c) reinvested at the discount rate.
(d) a diminishing return.

_____ 4 When considering incremental investment proposals with the internal-rate-of-discount method, one should accept a project if the _____

(a) incremental ρ is less than r.
(b) maximum value of ρ is different from the market rate of interest.
(c) incremental ρ is greater than r.
(d) incremental profitability index is greater than 1.

PROBLEMS FOR PRACTICE

1 What will be the value in six years of $75 compounded at 8%?

Solution

$W = S(1 + r)^n \qquad W = 75(1 + .08)^6 = 75(1.587) = \$119.02$

2 Determine the present value of a $1,000 bond with 15 years to maturity. The bond pays $75 annually in interest. The market rate of interest for equivalent risk, 15-year bonds is 8%.

Solution

(1) Present value of the 15 years of interest payments. (Refer to a table of the PV of an annuity of $1.) PV factor of $1 annually for 15 years discounted at 8% = 8.559.

$PV_1 = \$75 \times 8.559 = \$642$

(2) Present value of the $1,000 redemption in 15 years. (Refer to a table of the PV of $1.) PV factor of $1 in 15 years discounted at 8% = .315.

$PV_2 = \$1{,}000 \times .315 = \$315$

$PV = PV_1 + PV_2 = \$642 + \$315 = \$957$

3 Based on a 7% interest rate, calculate the present value of the following series of annual cash flows:

Years	*Cash Flow*
1–3	$5,000
4–5	8,000

Solution

(1) PV of $5,000 annually for years 1–3:

$5,000 × 2.624 = $13,120

(2) 4.100 PV of an annuity of $1 for 5 years at 7%
2.624 PV of an annuity of $1 for 3 years at 7%
1.476 PV of an annuity of $1 for years 4 and 5

$8,000 × 1.476 = $11,808

PV of total cash flows = $13,120 + $11,808 = $24,928

4 The winner of a lottery is offered two alternatives for collecting the prize money: (a) receive $1,000 per year for life or (b) receive $3,000 per year for four years. The winner is 20 years old and anticipates living to at least the age of 80. Ignoring any tax effect, which alternative should be selected when the discount rate is 12%.

Solution

(a) Sixty years of annual payments is approximated by a perpetuity.

$$PV = \frac{\$1{,}000}{.12} = \$8{,}333$$

(b) PV = \$3,000 × 3.037 = \$9,111

Since \$9,111 > \$8,333, alternative (b) is the proper choice

5 Fryer Company has a proposed investment project with an initial cost of \$8,500. The project is expected to yield a gross cash flow of \$3,000 annually for four years. The firm's rate of discount is 10%. Calculate the (a) net present value, (b) discounted gross benefit-cost ratio, and (c) internal rate of return.

Solution

(a) Net present value:

NPV = Σ PV of inflows − Σ PV of outflows

\$3,000 × 3.170 =	\$9,510	PV of inflows
\$8,500 × 1.000 =	8,500	PV of outflows
	\$1,010	NPV of project

(b) Discounted benefit-cost ratio (gross):

$$BCR = \frac{\text{PV of inflows}}{\text{PV of outflows}} = \frac{\$9{,}510}{\$8{,}500} = 1.119$$

(c) Internal rate of return:

14% Discount Rate		*16% Discount Rate*	
\$3,000 × 2.914 =	\$8,742	\$3,000 × 2.798 =	\$8,394
\$8,500 × 1.000 =	8,500	\$8,500 × 1.000 =	8,500
	\$ 242		\$ −106

IRR (approximate):

$$14.0\% + \frac{\$242}{242 + 106}(2.0\%) = 14.0 + 1.39 = 15.39\%$$

PROBLEMS FOR SELF-EXAMINATION

6 Compute the present value at a 12% discount rate of the following cash flows:

Year	*Cash Flow*
1	\$1,000
2	1,500
3	2,000
4	2,500
5	3,000

Solution

Year	*Discount Factor*	*Cash Flow*	*Discounted Cash Flow*
1		$1,000	$
2		1,500	
3	.712	2,000	1,424
4		2,500	
5		3,000	
			$6,804 PV of cash flows

7 A choice is offered between receiving $5,000 in six years or $6,000 in eight years. (a) Which is the proper choice if the discount rate is 8%? (b) If the discount rate is 12% instead, would you make the same decision?

Solution

(a) 8% discount rate:

$5,000 × .630 = $3,150 PV of cash flow

$6,000 × = $ PV of cash flow

The $____ payment is preferred because it yields the ____ PV.

(b) 12% discount rate:

$5,000 × = $ PV of cash flow

$6,000 × = $ PV of cash flow

The $____ payment is preferred because it yields the ____ PV.

8 A new molding machine will cost $42,000. The expected cash flows generated by the new machine are

Year	*Gross Cash Flow*
1	$20,000
2	15,000
3	10,000
4	5,000

The firm's cost of capital is 14%. Calculate the net present value and the gross and net discounted benefit-cost ratios for the investment in the new machine. Should this investment proposal be accepted?

Solution

Year	____	*Cash Flow*	*Discounted Cash Flow*
1		$	$
2			
3			
4		5,000	2,960
			$

NPV = $ − $ =

Gross BCR = $\frac{\$}{\$}$ =

Net BCR = =

Accept ____ reject ____ the investment proposal.

9 Compute the internal rate of return for the investment proposal listed in Problem 8. Based on this criteria, should the proposal be accepted?

Solution

Year	Cash Flow	Discount Factor 10%	Discount Factor ____	Discounted Cash Flow 10%	Discounted Cash Flow ____
1	$20,000	.909		$18,180	$
2	15,000				
3	10,000				
4	5,000				
				$	$
		PV of cash outflow =		−42,000	−42,000
				$	$

IRR (approximate):

% + $\frac{\quad}{\quad + \quad}$ (%) = + = %

Since % > or < 14% (cost of capital), accept or reject the proposal. (Cross out the incorrect words.)

10 Calculate the present value of a $1,000 bond that will mature in 10 years. The current market rate of interest for equivalent risk, 10-year bonds is 6%. The coupon rate of the bond is 8%.

Solution

(1)

(2)

11 A new investment opportunity promises the following cash flows:

Year	Cash Flow
1	$25,000
2	40,000
3	45,000
4	40,000
5	25,000

If our cost of capital is 12%, what is the maximum amount that you should pay to enter into this opportunity?

Solution

12 Fliers, Inc. is evaluating Projects 1 and 2. The following are pertinent to the analysis:

Initial Cost	
Project 1	*Project 2*
$20,000	$120,000

	Cash Flow	
Year	*Project 1*	*Project 2*
1	$15,000	$60,000
2	15,000	60,000
3	15,000	60,000

Rank the two projects in order of desirability by the net present value and the discounted gross benefit-cost ratio. Fliers, Inc. cost of capital is 10%.

Solution

Project 1:

Project 2:

Ranking:

13 Projects A and B are estimated to have the following cash flows:

Year	*A*	*B*
1	$10,000	$ 2,000
2	8,000	5,000
3	6,000	5,000
4		8,000
5		10,000

Both projects have an initial cost of $18,000. The firm's cost of capital is 10%. Rank the two projects by the net present value and the internal rate of return.

Solution

Project A:

Project B:

Ranking:

5 Capital-Budgeting Techniques: The Case of Risk

Theme Previously mentioned capital-budgeting techniques have all assumed the certainty of and independence among future cash flows. Chapter 5 discusses these restrictive assumptions and presents several approaches to resolve them.

I Cohen and Cyert have proposed some general characteristics that always exist in a decision situation.

A There are two or more alternative courses of action.

B The decision maker engages in overt search to discover all the possible alternatives.

C In a specific case, any of a number of outcomes may result from the decision maker's actions.

D A payoff function exists, which defines a partial ordering and the utility of the outcomes.

E The decision maker has some information regarding the possible outcomes of a given problem.

II The distinctions among certainty, risk, and uncertainty are explained below.

A Certainty versus risk and uncertainty:

1 Certainty is characterized by complete information and unique outcomes for each alternative.
2 Risk and uncertainty are characterized by incomplete knowledge and the expectation of more than one possible outcome.

B Risk versus uncertainty:

1 A risky situation is repetitive and possesses a frequency distribution.
2 Uncertainty prevails when a situation is not repetitive and, therefore, cannot be characterized by a frequency distribution.

III Another look at some capital-budgeting techniques.

A Payback method.

1 Its high acceptance has been attributed to three reasons:
(a) It is easy to compute and communicate.
(b) Management has a preference for clear, capital recovery dates.
(c) Management has a tendency toward nonmaximizing goals.
2 Businessmen who prefer a stable, short-run earnings pattern tend to favor payback.

(a) Although discounted cash-flow techniques are inclined to maximize the firm's market value in the long run, they also produce erratic, short-run earnings patterns.
(b) It appears that management is strongly averse to risk and has a preference for stable liquidity.

3 Discounted cash-flow techniques may be modified to account for management's attitude toward risk and liquidity.
(a) The benefits and costs of this approach are a matter of managerial preferences.
(b) This approach does not necessarily lead to share-price maximization.

B Net-present-value, internal-rate-of-discount, and discounted benefit-cost ratio methods.

1 These techniques assume the following:
(a) Knowledge of the company's cost of capital
(b) Certainty of cash flows
(c) Independence among cash flows

2 Net present value is inversely related to the discount rate.

3 When the NPV equals zero, the (external) discount rate used in calculating the NPV equals the internal rate of discount, and the discounted benefit-cost ratio equals 1.

4 When projects are not mutually exclusive and when only an "accept or reject" decision is required, all three methods give the same answer.

5 However, when ranking projects with different cash flows, these methods are likely to produce contradictions:
(a) The results depend upon what value one uses for the (external) rate of discount.
(b) The results depend upon the slope and shape of the present-value profiles.

C The reinvestment-rate criterion combines the internal and external rates of return.

1 This proposal suggests that the decision maker compound all flows to their terminal value by reinvesting all intermediate cash inflows at the external rate and utilizing the same rate for all intermediate cash outflows.

2 Some factors to consider when attempting to obtain correct and consistent project rankings are
(a) Comparison among alternative courses of action is a better way to make decisions than comparison among projects.
(b) When using the rate of return as the relevant index of profitability, measure the profitability by the per annum yield of each course of action from its inception to a common terminal date.
(c) When using the NPV method, employ the reinvestment rate as the discount factor. Furthermore, when comparing projects with different costs, use the profitability index method.

IV The concept of expected-return maximization substitutes expectations for uncertainty; instead of maximizing profits, one attempts to maximize expected profits or return.

A The goal of expected-return maximization is applicable where the following attributes are present:

1 The experiment is replicable and repetitive.
2 Successive observations of the process are independent of the preceding ones.
3 Possible outcomes are not extreme.

B Expected-value maximization requires the expected value of each possible outcome to be computed and directs the decision maker to choose the course of action with the largest expected value.

C The most serious argument against the use of this criterion is its tendency to ignore risk.

1 The investment with the highest return may also have the greatest risk.
2 As the St. Petersburg paradox exemplifies, a high expected return may be characterized by a low payoff probability.

V Since all probabilities used for decision purposes are subjective, one can treat uncertainty as measurable risk and develop probability-refined versions of some standard investment criteria.

A After one has formed the probability distributions of the various outcomes, he may use them to maximize expected net present value or expected internal rate of discount or to minimize the expected payback period.

B However, the usefulness of subjective probability distributions is heavily dependent upon how accurately the probability estimates reflect reality.

VI Three methods of risk reduction that explicitly consider the variability of future cash flows are certainty equivalents, cash-equivalent functions, and mean-variance diversification.

A Certainty equivalents are artificial variables that the decision maker would choose instead of some future, uncertain value.

1 The expected return from an investment is discounted by its riskiness.
2 The decision maker will consider a riskier choice only if the expected return is high enough to compensate him for the additional risk.

B Cash-equivalent functions are developed in terms of a reference contract, as an extension of the certainty equivalent method.

1 This function for an individual is found in the following manner:
(a) Have him specify the amount of money he would pay for a reference contract to play a game with some fixed probability of winning an amount of money.
(b) Repeat this process for various probability values, and then plot probability versus the amount he would pay for each respective reference contract.
2 If the individual makes his decisions on the basis of expected value, he is indifferent to risk; if he will pay an amount greater than the expected-value equivalent, he is a risk taker; if he will pay an amount less than the expected-value equivalent, he is a risk averter.
3 Cash-equivalent curves are drawn assuming the individual has consistent preferences and can precisely express his indifference between any two options.

C Mean-variance diversification is based on the idea that it is portfolios, and not individual projects, which define the real set of available investment opportunities.

1 It incorporates investment constraints through the use of mathematical programming.
2 It involves the measure of covariance or the interrelationships among expected returns.
3 It incorporates the selection of investment combinations that maximize expected return for any level of risk.

VII Under certain conditions, the net-present-value curve is not a monotonically decreasing function of the discount rate; it may be a polynomial.

A If the NPV curve is a polynomial in n terms, then it has n roots or multiple rates of return.

B Descartes' rule of signs states that the number of solutions in the allowable range of values is at most equal to the number of reversals of sign in the sequence of future cash flows.

C If one defines investment to include all future cash flows, then almost every investment has multiple rates of return.

QUESTIONS FOR SELF-EXAMINATION

True or False

_____ 1 Discounted cash-flow techniques tend to produce erratic, short-run earnings patterns.

_____ 2 A better way to make decisions is to compare alternative courses of action rather than projects.

____ 3 Expected-return maximization substitutes certainty for uncertainty.

____ 4 Certainty equivalents are artificial variables that the decision maker is indifferent to when compared to some future, uncertain value.

____ 5 Multiple rates of return are a sure indication that the decision maker has incorrectly specified an investment project.

____ 6 In a decision situation, only one outcome is possible as a result of the decision maker's actions.

____ 7 Uncertainty is characterized by the certainty of more than one possible outcome.

____ 8 No matter what value one uses for the (external) rate of discount, the three standard discounted cash-flow techniques all give the same answer and project rankings.

____ 9 The reinvestment-rate criterion compounds all cash flows to their terminal value with the internal rate of discount.

____ 10 The tendency of the expected-value maximization criterion to disregard risk is critical.

Multiple Choice

____ 1 The usefulness of a subjective probability distribution is heavily dependent upon ____

(a) its standard deviation.
(b) the situation the distribution describes.
(c) its range of values.
(d) how accurately it reflects reality.

____ 2 The expected return from an investment is discounted by its ____

(a) profitability index.
(b) internal rate of discount.
(c) riskiness.
(d) subjectivity.

____ 3 If an individual is willing to pay \$100 so that he may play a game with a .70 probability of winning \$200, then he may be described as ____

(a) a risk averter.
(b) a risk taker.
(c) indifferent to risk.
(d) reckless.

____ 4 Mean-variance diversification is based on the idea that it is ____ which define the real set of investment opportunities.

(a) probability distributions
(b) multiple rates of return
(c) investment combinations
(d) individual investment projects

____ 5 If an investment project has an initial outlay of \$100,000, expected yearly inflows for three years of \$50,000, and a final outflow of \$10,000, then according to Descartes' rule of signs there will be ____ rates of return.

(a) three
(b) two
(c) at most three
(d) at most two

PROBLEMS FOR PRACTICE

1 The E. Z. Service Company is preparing its annual capital budget. Two proposed projects, A and B, have initial costs of \$22,000 and \$32,500, respectively. Their estimated cash flows are

Year	*A*	*B*
1	$10,000	$10,000
2	8,000	10,000
3	8,000	12,000
4	6,000	15,000

The company's cost of capital is 8%. Rank these two projects by their net present value, discounted gross benefit-cost ratio, and internal rate of return.

Solution

Project A:

Year	*Cash Flow*	*Discount Factor* 8%	*Discounted Cash Flow* 8%
1	$10,000	.926	$ 9,260
2	8,000	.857	6,856
3	8,000	.794	6,352
4	6,000	.735	4,410
			$26,878
			−22,000
		NPV =	$ 4,878

$$\text{BCR} = \frac{\$26{,}878}{\$22{,}000} = 1.222$$

Year	*Cash Flow*	*Discount Factor* 18%	*Discount Factor* 20%	*Discounted Cash Flow* 18%	*Discounted Cash Flow* 20%
1	$10,000	.847	.833	$ 8,470	$ 8,330
2	8,000	.718	.694	5,744	5,552
3	8,000	.609	.579	4,872	4,632
4	6,000	.516	.482	3,096	2,892
				$22,182	$21,406
				−22,000	−22,000
				$ 182	$ −594

IRR (approximate):

$$18.0\% + \frac{\$182}{182 + 594}(2.0\%) = 18.0 + .47 = 18.47\%$$

Project B:

Year	*Cash Flow*	*Discount Factor* 8%	*Discounted Cash Flow* 8%
1	$10,000	.926	$ 9,260
2	10,000	.857	8,570
3	12,000	.794	9,528
4	15,000	.735	11,025
			$38,383
			−32,500
		NPV =	$ 5,883

$$\text{BCR} = \frac{\$38{,}383}{\$32{,}500} = 1.181$$

Year	Cash Flow	Discount Factor 14%	Discount Factor 16%	Discounted Cash Flow 14%	Discounted Cash Flow 16%
1	$10,000	.877	.862	$ 8,770	$ 8,620
2	10,000	.769	.743	7,690	7,430
3	12,000	.675	.641	8,100	7,692
4	15,000	.592	.552	8,880	8,280
				$33,440	$32,022
				−32,500	−32,500
				$ 940	$ −478

IRR (approximate):

$$14.0\% + \frac{\$940}{940 + 478}(2.0\%) = 14.0 + 1.33 = 15.33\%$$

Ranking:[1]

NPV	*BCR*	*IRR*
Project B	Project A	Project A
Project A	Project B	Project B

[1] Note the inconsistency in the rankings.

2 Jim Student has the choice of accepting a job as manager of a new fast food outlet or an established local restaurant. In both positions he will be paid a percentage of total receipts. The amount of business conducted by each establishment is associated with general economic conditions. After careful consideration, Jim has estimated the probability of future economic conditions and the income received from each position. Help Jim choose the position that will maximize his expected income.

Income	*Economic Conditions* Slump (.10)	No Growth (.30)	Steady Growth (.40)	Rapid Growth (.20)
Fast Food	$1,000	$ 7,000	$18,000	$24,000
Restaurant	8,000	12,000	15,000	18,000

Solution

Fast Food:

$1,000 (.10) + $7,000 (.30) + $18,000 (.40) + $24,000 (.20) = $14,200

Restaurant:

$8,000 (.10) + $12,000 (.30) + $15,000 (.40) + $18,000 (.20) = $14,000

Since $14,200 > $14,000, Jim should accept the manager's job at the fast food outlet.

3 A new machine costs $56,000. Its future cash flows depend upon the sales demand for its output. The financial manager projects a 20% chance of $10,000 per year cash flow, a 50% chance of $23,000 per year cash flow, and a 30% chance of $30,000 per year cash flow. The company uses a three-year horizon, and its cost of capital is 10%. Employing the expected-net-present-value criterion, what will management decide?

Solution

Cash Flow		PV Cash Flow		Cost				Probability		E(NPV_i)
\$10,000 ×	2.487 =	\$24,870	−	\$56,000 =	\$−31,130	×	.20 =			\$−6,226
\$23,000 ×	2.487 =	\$57,201	−	\$56,000 =	\$ 1,201	×	.50 =			601
\$30,000 ×	2.487 =	\$74,610	−	\$56,000 =	\$ 18,610	×	.30 =			5,583
							Expected NPV	= \$		−42

Since E(NPV) = \$−42 < 0, the proposal will be rejected.

4 A return of 12% and risk of .07 (variance) is the certainty equivalent of a return of 18% and risk of .19 (variance). What is the certainty-equivalent return at zero risk with a linear certainty-equivalent function?

Solution

$$\frac{18\% - 12\%}{(.19 - .07)/.01} = \frac{6\%}{12} = .5\% \text{ return per .01 unit of risk}$$

$$12.0\% - \frac{.07}{.01} \times .5\% = 12.0 - 3.5 = 8.5\% \text{ return at zero risk}$$

PROBLEMS FOR SELF-EXAMINATION

5 Two investment opportunities, C and D, are available. Investment C is speculative and exhibits wider fluctuations in its returns than the stock market averages. In contrast, Investment D is conservative and fluctuates moderately. The anticipated performance of the stock market with its probabilities of occurrence and the associated returns for each investment are

	Stock Market Performance			
Return	*10% Decline (.05)*	*No Change (.50)*	*10% Increase (.35)*	*20% Increase (.10)*
Investment C	−15%	0%	15%	30%
Investment D	0%	5%	10%	15%

If maximizing expected return is your decision criterion, which investment is the proper choice?

Solution

Investment C:

$$E(\text{return}) = -15(\quad) + 0(\quad) + 15(\quad) + 30(\quad)$$
$$= -.75 \quad + \quad + \quad +$$
$$= \quad \%$$

Investment D:

$$E(\text{return}) = 0(\quad) + 5(\quad) + 10(\quad) + 15(\quad)$$
$$= 0 \quad + \quad + \quad +$$
$$= \quad \%$$

Select Investment _____ .

6 Your partner suggests expanding your joint candle-making enterprise. The first alternative costs \$40,000 and will generate cash flows of \$15,000 per year for the next four years. The second

possibility requires $60,000 and will generate cash flows of $23,000 per year for four consecutive years. However, because of special training needed, the cash flows for the second project will not begin until the second year. Utilizing an 8% cost of capital, recommend one of the expansion alternatives on the basis of (a) net present value, (b) benefit-cost ratio, and (c) internal rate of return.

Solution

7 The financial manager of Smoothy Company obtained the following data for two projects, E and F. The two projects require initial outlays of $85,000 and $125,000, respectively. The company's cost of capital is 10%. Based on the expected-net-present-value criterion, which project should be selected?

Project E		*Project F*	
Probability	*Annual Cash Flow*	*Probability*	*Annual Cash Flow*
.20	$30,000 for 3 years	.10	$32,000 for 4 years
.30	25,000 for 4 years	.40	30,000 for 5 years
.40	30,000 for 4 years	.30	35,000 for 5 years
.10	35,000 for 4 years	.20	40,000 for 5 years

Solution

Project E:

Project F:

8 For each of the above two projects, E and F, the approximate internal rate of return for each of the four possible patterns of annual cash flow are Project E, 2.94%, 6.85%, 15.39%, and 23.44%, respectively; Project F, .96%, 6.41%, 12.40%, and 18.03%, respectively. Using the expected internal rate of return, will the decision of Smoothy Company be the same?

Solution

9 Jim Broke selects risky investments on the basis of a linear certainty-equivalent function. Jim has determined that for him a return of 14.5% and risk of .08 is the certainty equivalent of a 9% return and risk of .04. His brother has offered him the opportunity to invest risk free and obtain a return of 3%. Assuming Jim behaves rationally, will he invest in this opportunity?

Solution

6 Interdependence and Uncertainty in Investment Decisions

Theme Chapter 6 confronts the problems of uncertainty, capital scarcity, the interdependence among investment projects, and risk reduction.

I Three major components cause uncertainty in business decisions:

A Uncertainty of economic parameters.

B Uncertainty of domestic and international political developments.

C Uncertainty of one's environment and its constraints.

II In a broad sense, economic uncertainty derives from the market place and the utility function of the decision maker.

A Market place uncertainty encompasses business, financial, and portfolio risks.

1 Business risk reflects the uncertainty of the firm's profits due to product and labor market influences.
2 Financial risk reflects the uncertainty of the firm's economic position due to money and capital market influences.
3 Portfolio risk reflects the uncertainty due to interrelationships and interactions of returns from investment proposals.

B The uncertainty of the utility function of the decision maker can occur through incorrect specification or estimation.

III The sequential acceptance procedure for investment-proposal rankings introduces the problems of capital scarcity and the indivisibility of investment projects.

A Capital rationing is the allocation of the firm's budgeted (scarce) investment funds among the most desirable projects.

B Since investments in plant and equipment are typically all-or-none propositions, the indivisibility of investment projects is a serious problem.

1 As projects are accepted in ranked order, investment opportunities may be encountered whose costs are greater than the remaining budgeted funds.
2 Scaled-down or reduced investments may entail unpleasant consequences, or they may be altogether infeasible.

IV Another analytical difficulty inherent in investment decisions is the interdependence among investment proposals.

A Proposals are mutually exclusive if the decision maker can accept only one of them and must exclude the others.

B Proposals are mutually dependent (contingent) if a project cannot be undertaken without another.

V Lorie and Savage view the problem of capital rationing as encompassing two types of investment decisions: the selection among independent alternatives and the selection among interdependent alternatives.

A The selection among independent alternatives may be further classified.

1 Single-period investments should be ranked using the profitability index and selected in decreasing order of index magnitude.
(a) In the absence of project indivisibility and interdependence, this procedure maximizes the present value of the owners' equity.
(b) However, when confronted with the problem of indivisibility, this technique fails.
2 Multiperiod investments, of which there are two possible subcases, involve the possibility of multiple rates of return.
(a) The budget constraint may be binding only during the first time period.
(b) The budget constraint may be binding for more than one time period.

B The selection among interdependent alternatives is more complicated than the above case.

1 There are two possible subcases:
(a) The mutual dependence among new investment proposals.
(b) The dependence of the existing and the new assets in terms of the variability of their future flows.
2 Interdependence encompasses three broad classifications:
(a) Structural interdependence, which arises from the pattern of interactions between firms and industries.
(b) Macroeconomic interdependence, which arises from the cohesive nature of economic variables.
(c) Demographic interdependence, which arises from the social structure of the economy.

VI Techniques for discounting risk properly in capital-budgeting decisions include practical, conceptual, and probabilistic methods.

A Practical methods.

1 The finite-horizon method is similar to the payback-period approach.
(a) It involves the assignment of a terminal date to the investment proposal.
(b) The distinction, however, is that the finite-horizon method is concerned with long time periods and distant investment horizons.
2 Risk-discounting methods, two of which appear below, combine the adjustment of an expected cash flow for risk as well as for futurity.
(a) Discount the estimated cash flows of the different projects at rates corresponding to each project's riskiness.
(i) A serious limitation is that investment selection is not neutral to the discount rate.
(ii) A change in the discount rate may change the ranking of the projects.
(b) An alternative procedure allows one to adjust directly the estimated cash flows in each future time period.
3 Sensitivity analysis is not really a risk-reduction technique; it tests the robustness of a model by determining how changes or errors in parameter values affect the output.

B A conceptual method.

1 Professor Shackle argues that decision makers tend to characterize the risk of an investment decision in terms of two extreme outcomes: *focus gain*, a representative potential gain, and *focus loss*, a representative potential loss.

2 Shackle's technique is presented in terms of the *potential surprise* that an unexpected outcome gives the decision maker.
3 His approach is totally reliant on subjective probabilities.

C Probabilistic methods (for the analysis of single projects).

1 The rationale for probabilistic methods is that since the expected future returns from an investment decision under uncertainty are random variables, their net present value will also be a random variable. Following are two examples of this capital-budgeting approach:
2 The Hillier model is intended as a complement to existing evaluation procedures.
   (a) Develop the probability distribution of the net present value of each investment proposal.
   (b) Derive the expected value and variance of the above distribution.
   (c) Cognizant of this information, select the project most consistent with one's decision criterion.
3 The Hertz model is a simulation experiment that incorporates risk analysis in the investment decisions of the firm, via the use of value ranges and probability weighting.
   (a) It involves a number of interlocking stages.
      (i) Estimate the range of values and the likelihood of occurrence for each relevant variable.
      (ii) Using statistical sampling techniques, select a specific value for each variable, combine all values, and compute the outcome according to some investment criterion.
      (iii) Repeat stage (ii) for a predetermined number of iterations. Compute the average expected outcome by weighting each outcome according to its probability of occurrence.
      (iv) Having computed the average expected outcome and its variance for each proposal, use this information in conjunction with the firm's decision criterion.
   (b) Hertz uses three categories of input variables:
      (i) Market analysis variables, which generate different values for expected sales revenue.
      (ii) Investment-costs analysis variables, which include technological factors that are a source of uncertainty in the decision process.
      (iii) Operating- and fixed-costs analysis variables, which include information about the firm's production function.

QUESTIONS FOR SELF-EXAMINATION

True or False

_____ 1 If it were not for capital scarcity, there would not be a need for capital rationing.

_____ 2 When confronted with the indivisibility problem, single-period investments involve the possibility of multiple rates of return.

_____ 3 Macroeconomic interdependence arises from the cohesiveness of economic variables.

_____ 4 Sensitivity analysis is presented in terms of the potential surprise that an unexpected outcome gives the decision maker.

_____ 5 The indivisibility of investment projects means that a project cannot be undertaken without another.

_____ 6 The selection among interdependent alternatives concerns the dependence among new investment proposals and between new and existing assets.

_____ 7 The covariance of project returns is a critical concern when one is choosing among independent alternatives.

_____ 8 The Hillier and the Hertz models both complement existing evaluation procedures.

_____ 9 Risk-discounting methods discount for futurity and risk.

_____ 10 The finite-horizon method assigns a payback period to each investment proposal.

Multiple Choice

_____ 1 Uncertainty in the market place comprises _____ risk.
(a) portfolio
(b) financial
(c) business
(d) all the above

_____ 2 Proposals are _____ if the decision maker must accept only one among several alternatives.
(a) infeasible
(b) mutually exclusive
(c) single-period investments
(d) mutually dependent

_____ 3 The _______ is a simulation experiment that incorporates risk analysis in the investment decision.
(a) Hertz model
(b) Shackle conceptual method
(c) Hoskold method
(d) Hillier model

_____ 4 Shackle's technique is totally reliant on _______
(a) surprises.
(b) random variables.
(c) subjective probabilities.
(d) simulation.

_____ 5 The Hertz and Hillier models are both examples of _______ for capital-budgeting decisions.
(a) conceptual methods
(b) probabilistic methods
(c) practical methods
(d) certainty methods

PROBLEMS FOR PRACTICE

1 Machine Products has prepared its capital budget for the coming year. Six projects are deemed desirable; however, their total initial cost is $235,000, but only $125,000 of capital funds are available. The company also may invest in government bonds yielding 5%. The data concerning the six projects are detailed below. (a) If all projects are completely divisible, what projects will be selected, and what is their average benefit-cost ratio? (b) If the projects are not divisible, what is the optimum selection of projects based on the average benefit-cost ratio?

Project	*Benefit-cost Ratio*	*Initial Cost*
1	1.55	$ 40,000
2	1.43	10,000
3	1.36	35,000
4	1.26	100,000
5	1.18	20,000
6	1.16	30,000

Solution

(a) The first three projects are accepted to their limit. \$40,000/\$100,000 = 40% of the fourth project is selected.

$$\text{Avg. BCR} = \frac{\$\ 40{,}000}{\$125{,}000}(1.55) + \frac{\$\ 10{,}000}{\$125{,}000}(1.43) + \frac{\$\ 35{,}000}{\$125{,}000}(1.36) + \frac{\$\ 40{,}000}{\$125{,}000}(1.26)$$

$$= .496 + .114 + .381 + .403$$

$$= 1.394$$

(b) Partial projects are not permissible. The remaining funds will be invested in government bonds at a BCR of 1.05.

Selection 1: Projects 1, 2, 3, 5

$$\text{Avg. BCR} = .496 + .114 + .381 + \frac{\$\ 20{,}000}{\$125{,}000}(1.18) + \frac{\$\ 20{,}000}{\$125{,}000}(1.05)$$

$$= 1.348$$

Selection 2: Projects 1, 2, 3, 6

$$\text{Avg. BCR} = .496 + .114 + .381 + \frac{\$\ 30{,}000}{\$125{,}000}(1.16) + \frac{\$\ 10{,}000}{\$125{,}000}(1.05)$$

$$= 1.354$$

Selection 2 is preferred because of its higher average BCR.

2 The Bishop Company is considering two mutually exclusive projects. Project 1 costs \$45,000 and is expected to generate annual cash flows of \$15,000 for five years. Project 2 is anticipated to produce annual cash flows of \$39,000 for six years with an initial cost of \$145,000. Currently the company's cost of capital is 10%. The risk associated with Project 1 is equivalent to the current riskiness of the company; thus the discount rate employed with the project is 10%. It is the consensus of the finance committee, however, that a risk factor of 4% should be applied to Project 2. (a) Using NPV, which project is the appropriate selection? (b) If the increased riskiness of Project 2 were ignored, which project would be selected?

Solution

(a) *Project 1 at 10% discount rate*

\$15,000 × 3.791 = \$56,865
−45,000
NPV = \$11,865

Project 2 at 14% discount rate

\$39,000 × 3.889 = \$151,671
−145,000
NPV = \$ 6,671

Since \$11,865 > \$6,671, Project 1 is selected.

(b) *Project 2 at 10% discount rate*

\$39,000 × 4.355 = \$169,845
−145,000
NPV = \$ 24,845

Ignoring the increased riskiness, Project 2 is selected.

7 Cost of Capital from Specific Sources

Theme The cost of capital is a central concept of the financial management program and will be developed in terms of the availability and costs of various sources of funds.

I Productive assets are acquired with internal funds, external funds, or a combination of the two.

A Internal sources of capital are those that are generated from the current operations of the firm.

1 There are two internal sources of funds:
(a) The reinvestment of retained earnings enables the firm to pursue growth opportunities, as constrained by the amount of plowback.
(b) Depreciation reserves provide for replacement investment.

2 Exclusive reliance on internal sources of funds may lead to one of three situations:
(a) If a firm engages in continuous replacement through depreciation reserves, at the same rate of return and without other investments, the firm will remain stationary in size.
(b) If the assets of a firm are growing through the reinvestment of earnings (or other sources), but the rate of return is constant, the firm is on an expansion path.
(c) If the asset base is growing and the rate of return from new investments is greater than that from existing assets, the firm is on a growth path.

B External sources of funds arise from the sale of financial claims, based on the anticipated earnings of the firm.

1 The four major sources of long-term, external financing are
(a) Bonds
(b) Common stock
(c) Preferred stock
(d) Convertible securities

2 The size and composition of these claims, together with internal financing policies, determine the firm's capital structure.

3 Financial claims are generally classified into equity instruments, held by stockholders, and debt instruments, held by creditors.
(a) The creditors of a firm have a prior claim over the equity owners on the income stream of the firm.
(b) In cases of business failure, creditors have a prior claim over equity owners on the assets of the firm.
(c) Creditors usually have a fixed and rigidly specified claim on income, whereas common stockholders have a claim on residual earnings.

(d) Stockholders have the right to vote for the board of directors; creditors do not have any voting rights but do impose restrictions on the firm.
(e) Although the interest payments, the issue expense, and the amortization discount on debt are all deductible for corporate income tax purposes, dividend payments are considered as a distribution of profits and cannot be deducted.

II The cost of capital, K, is the rate of return necessary to maintain the wealth of the firm's owners.

A It is the basic measure of financial performance and is used to determine the acceptability of all investment opportunities.

B The cost of capital is a controversial issue, and a large part of its conceptual difficulty emanates from the uncertainty of cash flows and the variety of financial instruments.

C Under conditions of perfect certainty, the cost of capital is equal to the market rate of interest; that is, $K = i$.

1 All proposals offering a rate of return greater than the cost of capital, the interest rate, should be accepted.
2 The cost of capital serves as a cutoff point that delineates the set of acceptable investment opportunities.

D In the real world of market uncertainty, the interest rate is not a sufficient measure of the cost of capital.

1 Whereas the expected returns from a project are subject to uncertainty, the contractual costs of the project are certain and rigidly specified.
2 A realistic measure of the cost of capital should possess the following attributes:
(a) It must account for proposal uncertainty.
(b) It must allow for the various degrees of uncertainty associated with the firm's different uses of funds.
(c) It must allow for the covariances within a portfolio.
(d) It must account for the various means of financing.
(e) It must allow for the variable effects of different financing combinations.
(f) It must reflect changes in the capital markets.

E The cost of capital may be divided into an explicit and an implicit component.

1 The explicit cost of capital is the discount rate that equates the present values of the incremental cash inflows and outflows associated with a financing opportunity.
(a) It is the minimum required rate of return from an investment opportunity.
(b) Under this artificial concept, retained earnings, depreciation charges, and other noncash charges may be treated as windfalls or gifts and, hence, may be assigned an explicit cost of capital of negative 100%.
2 The implicit cost of capital, an opportunity cost concept, is the rate of return associated with the best alternative investment opportunity.

III Considerations of the cost of external equity appear below.

A The basic equation for Solomon's dynamic growth model is

$$P = D/K_e + Pb\epsilon$$

where P = market value of a share of common stock
D = dividend per share
K_e = stockholder's capitalization rate or external cost of capital
b = retention rate of firm
$\epsilon = r/K_e$ where r is rate of return promised by new investments, with $\epsilon > 1$

B With the appropriate assumptions, the model reduces to

$$P = D/K_e$$
$$P = E/K_e$$
$$K_e = E/P$$

where E = earnings per share

1 These assumptions are as follows:
   (a) The depreciation expenses of the firm just allow the firm's earnings to remain constant.
   (b) New investment returns are independent of the present returns of the firm.
   (c) The firm pays out all its earnings as dividends; that is, $b = 0$ and $D = E$.
2 These assumptions ensure that any change which occurs in the capitalization rate of stockholders will be caused by a change in the financial risk of the firm.
3 The reduced model states that the market value of a share of common stock is a multiple, $1/K_e$, of the firm's earnings per share.

C Dilution of earnings is the drop in earnings per share caused by the issuance of more common stock — an expansion of the firm's equity base.

1 One attempts to prevent earnings dilution by investing only in projects with a rate of return greater than or equal to the capitalization rate.
2 However, the dilution of earnings can occur as a result of the time lag between the sale of new stock and the first cash inflows of the financed project.

D Disregarding privileged subscriptions, dilution of control is the weakening of the original shareholders' voting power as a result of the issuance of new stock.

IV Considerations of the cost of internal equity appear below.

A The firm should retain earnings, i.e., withhold dividends, only when it can invest these earnings in projects promising to earn at least the cost of capital.

B The investment-opportunities approach to security valuation states that payout is a dependent variable inversely related to the firm's investment opportunities, the independent variable.

1 As long as acceptable investment opportunities exist, the firm should retain all its earnings.
2 However, actual dividend policy tends to be quite rigid, as if management has a target payout ratio that is gradually adjusted for changes in earnings.
   (a) Stockholders probably prefer a regular stream of dividend payments.
   (b) Debt is viewed as a much cheaper source of funds than equity.
   (c) Above-average investment opportunities are the exception rather than the rule.

C If one relaxes the third assumption and allows $b > 0$, then the earnings of the firm do grow.

1 The capitalization rate is now the sum of the dividend yield and the growth rate of the firm; that is, $K_e = D/P + br$.
2 In general, the capitalization rate for growth firms is greater than that for nongrowth firms.

V The dividend policy of the firm involves the conflicting interests of different groups of shareholders.

A The irrelevance of dividends hypothesis states that as long as a viable market for securities exists, the investment and consumption opportunities of the shareholders are not relevant to the firm's financial decisions.

1 If dissatisfied, a stockholder may sell his holdings in the firm and invest elsewhere.

2 If satisfied or if the shareholder's investment opportunities are less than that of the firm, he may reinvest his dividends in the firm.

B If the firm wishes to maximize per share market price and the owners' wealth, then it should attempt to maximize the sum of the current dividends paid and the ex-dividend price of the common stock.

1 The firm should pay a dividend if the resultant price decline in the common stock is less than the amount of the dividend.

2 In marginal terms, the planned current dividend per share should be increased to the point where the last increment results in an equal decline in the ex-dividend price of the common stock.

VI The cost of debt capital is the rate of return from debt-financed projects necessary to maintain the wealth of the firm's owners.

A If a firm finances with debt, *ceteris paribus*, it increases both the expected returns of the firm and the risk of these returns.

B Leverage or trading on the equity is the utilization of debt capital to invest in projects that promise a return greater than the fixed debt payments.

1 Although the expected return to the owners is larger for the firm when it uses leverage than when it does not, the variability of expected returns is also larger.

2 If the firm acquires too much debt, then the value of its equity may decrease due to the burden of financial risk.

QUESTIONS FOR SELF-EXAMINATION

True or False

_____ 1 External sources of funds arise from the sale of financial claims.

_____ 2 The reinvestment of depreciation reserves provides the firm with an opportunity for growth.

_____ 3 A fixed and rigidly specified claim on income is a common characteristic of creditors to the firm.

_____ 4 The market rate of interest is usually a good approximation of the cost of capital.

_____ 5 The implicit cost of capital is the rate of return associated with the best alternative investment opportunity.

_____ 6 The capitalization rate of stockholders is directly related to the financial risk of the firm.

_____ 7 The dilution of earnings and the dilution of control are both caused by the expansion of the equity base of the firm.

_____ 8 Debt is viewed as a much more expensive source of funds than equity.

_____ 9 Trading on the equity is the use of equity capital to invest in projects that promise an acceptable rate of return.

_____ 10 The employed combination of the internal and external sources of funds is the capital structure of the firm.

_____ 11 The cost of capital is concerned only with the business risk of the firm.

_____ 12 The increase in the variability of expected returns through the use of leverage is often a more important consideration than the increase in the expected return to the firm's owners.

Multiple Choice

_____ 1 If the asset base of a firm is growing and the rate of return from new investments is greater than that from existing assets, then the firm ________
- (a) is on an expansion path.
- (b) is on a growth path.
- (c) will remain stationary in size.
- (d) has little business risk.

_____ 2 Which of the following is not one of the four major sources of long-term, external financing?
- (a) Long-term bank loans
- (b) Common Stock
- (c) Preferred stock
- (d) Bonds

_____ 3 Which of the following is not characteristic of the creditors of a firm?
- (a) A prior claim over owners to assets
- (b) The right to impose restrictive conditions on the firm
- (c) A fixed claim on income
- (d) A right to vote for the board of directors

_____ 4 A reduced form of Solomon's dynamic growth model is ________ .
- (a) $P = r/K_e$
- (b) $K_e = E/P$
- (c) $K_e = P/b$
- (d) $P = b/K_e$

_____ 5 The firm should retain all its earnings if ________
- (a) interest on debt must be paid.
- (b) the cost of external capital is high.
- (c) it wants to maximize the wealth of its owners.
- (d) acceptable investment opportunities exist.

PROBLEMS FOR PRACTICE

1 Two $1,000 bonds have the same 6% contractual (coupon) rate of interest. However, the maturity of the first bond is 10 years and the second is 20 years. (a) If both bonds are currently selling for $1,000, what are their respective rates of return? (b) If both bond prices decline to $800, how do their rates of return change?

Solution

(a) Since the current market price of the bond is equal to its maturity value, the rate of return for each bond is equal to the coupon rate of 6%.

(b) The rate of return is determined by trial and error.

10-year bond at 8%

$ 60	× 6.710	=	$402.60
1,000	× .463	=	463.00
			$865.60

20-year bond at 8%

$ 60	× 9.818	=	$589.08
1,000	× .215	=	215.00
			$804.08

10-year bond at 10%

$ 60	× 6.145	=	$368.70
1,000	× .386	=	386.00
			$754.70

Rate of return (approximate) = 8%

Rate of return (approximate):

$$8.0\% + \frac{866 - 800}{866 - 755}(2.0\%) = 8.0 + 1.19 = 9.19\%$$

Note the inverse relationship between the bond prices and the rates of return. Also note that for a \$200 decrease in the bond price, the longer term bond experienced a smaller increase in its rate of return.

2 The Golden Company is planning on raising \$180,000 by issuing additional common stock. Currently a share of common stock of Golden is selling at \$45, which represents a *P/E* ratio of 12. One of the company's objectives is to avoid dilution of the earnings of the existing stockholders. Because of this, they are able to sell new stock at the current market price. (a) Ignoring flotation costs, what is the required rate of return for the new investment? (b) Determine the required rate of return if flotation costs are \$3 per share.

Solution

(a) $\frac{\$45}{12}$ = \$3.67 earnings per share for existing shareholders

$\frac{\$180,000}{\$45}$ = 4,000 new shares

\$3.67 × 4,000 shares = \$14,680 return necessary from new investment

$\frac{\$\ 14,680}{\$180,000}$ = 8.16% required rate of return

(b) \$45 − \$3 = \$42 proceeds per new share sold

$\frac{\$180,000}{\$42}$ = 4,286 new shares

\$3.67 × 4,286 shares = \$15,730 return necessary from new investment

$\frac{\$\ 15,730}{\$180,000}$ = 8.74% required rate of return

3 A share of common stock of Company A is selling for \$50 at a *P/E* ratio of 12.5. There are 250,000 shares outstanding, and the company practices a passive dividend policy. The company is considering a project that requires an investment of 25% of the annual earnings. (a) Ignoring the personal income tax effect, calculate the stockholders wealth if the project is not undertaken. (b) Determine the stockholders wealth if the project is accepted and returns 6% or 10% of net earnings.

Solution

$\frac{\$50}{12.5}$ = \$4.00 earnings per share

\$4.00 × 250,000 shares = \$1 million total earnings

\$1,000,000 × .25 = \$250,000 project cost

\$4.00 × .75 = \$3.00 dividend per share

$K_e = E/P = \frac{4.00}{50}$ = 8% capitalization rate

(a) Payout = 100%

Stockholders wealth: \$50.00 market value
4.00 dividend
\$54.00

(b) Payout = 75%, project accepted

	r = 6%	r = 10%
Current earnings	\$1,000,000	\$1,000,000
Incremental earnings from project	15,000	25,000
Total earnings	\$1,015,000	\$1,025,000
Earnings per share	\$4.06	\$4.10
Capitalization rate, K_e	.08	.08
Market value of common	\$50.75	\$51.25
Dividend paid	3.00	3.00
Total stockholders wealth	\$53.75	\$54.25

4 Grass, Inc. is obtaining from current operations \$150,000 earnings before interest and taxes. It has 100,000 shares of common stock outstanding, and its marginal tax rate is 40%. To invest in a \$300,000 project, Grass, Inc. has to acquire the necessary funds. It is able to issue either 8% bonds or additional common stock at \$10 per share. Determine the resultant earnings per share from the alternative financing plans if the project returns EBIT of 10%, 16%, or 20% on investment.

Solution

Debt financing:

\$300,000 × .08 = \$24,000 interest

Equity financing:

$$\frac{\$300{,}000}{\$10} = 30{,}000 \text{ additional shares}$$

	Debt Financing (thousands)		
	r = 10%	r = 16%	r = 20%
Current EBIT	\$150	\$150	\$150
Incremental EBIT	30	48	60
Total EBIT	\$180	\$198	\$210
Interest	24	24	24
Taxable income	\$156	\$174	\$186
Taxes (40%)	62	70	74
Net income	\$ 94	\$104	\$112
EPS (100,000 shares)	\$.94	\$1.04	\$1.12

	Stock Financing (thousands)		
	r = 10%	r = 16%	r = 20%
Total EBIT and taxable income	\$180	\$198	\$210
Taxes (40%)	72	79	84
Net income	\$108	\$119	\$126
EPS (130,000 shares)	\$.83	\$.92	\$.96

With the above percentage returns, the financial leverage of debt financing is favorable. The range of EPS for debt financing is \$.18 and the range for stock financing is \$.13. Thus the financial leverage increases the variability of the EPS.

5 An objective of the J. B. Brown Company is to maintain the market value of its common stock

whenever it enters into a new investment. It has available a $200,000 project that can be financed with 8% bonds. The company's 150,000 shares of common stock are currently priced at $65 per share. The market is capitalizing this equity at 12%. (a) Assuming the capitalization rate remains constant, what is the required rate of return for the project? (b) Because of the increased debt, the capitalization rate increases to 12.5%. Determine the new required rate of return for the project.

Solution

(a) $K_e = .12$

EPS = .12 × $65 = $7.80

Required earnings (after tax) = $7.80 × 150,000 shares = $1,170,000

Interest (after tax) = $200,000 × .08 (1 – .4) = $9,600

Total required earnings = $1,170,000 + $9,600 = $1,179,600

Current earnings = .12 × $65 × 150,000 shares = $1,170,000

Earnings required of project = $1,179,600 – $1,170,000 = $9,600

$$\text{Required rate of return} = \frac{\$\ \ 9{,}600}{\$200{,}000} = .048 = 4.8\%$$

(b) $K_e = .125$

EPS = .125 × $65 = $8.125

Required earnings (after tax) = $8.125 × 150,000 shares = $1,218,750

Interest (after tax) = $9,600

Total required earnings = $1,218,750 + $9,600 = $1,228,350

Current earnings = $1,170,000

Earnings required of project = $1,228,350 – $1,170,000 = $58,350

$$\text{Required rate of return} = \frac{\$\ 58{,}350}{\$200{,}000} = .292 = 29.2\%$$

PROBLEMS FOR SELF-EXAMINATION

6 A $1,000 bond with a 7% contractual (coupon) rate of interest has a market price of $1,125. With a maturity of 15 years, what is the rate of return for the bond?

Solution

PV of inflow = $

PV of outflows

4% Rate of Return		*6% Rate of Return*	
$ 70 ×	= $	$ 70 ×	= $
1,000 × .555 =	______	1,000 ×	= ______
	$		$

Rate of return (approximate):

$$4.0\% + \frac{\quad - \quad}{\quad - \quad}\;(\qquad) = \qquad + \qquad = \qquad \%$$

7 If the price of the $1,000, 15-year bond in Problem 6 declines to $875, what is its new rate of return?

Solution

8 The Worth Company is anticipating a major expansion costing \$600,000. The necessary funds may be obtained by selling common stock at the current market price or by issuing bonds yielding 9% interest. The company has no existing debt and expects to generate net earnings of \$2 per share on the 48,000 outstanding shares of common stock. The *P/E* ratio is 25 and the marginal tax rate is 40%. Which financing alternative is preferable if the expansion returns 15% or 20% EBIT on investment?

Solution

8 The Combined Cost of Capital

Theme Chapter 8 presents some of the complications that arise when a firm combines several sources of funds to finance its investment opportunities.

I The problems raised by a financing mix have been classified by Solomon into four areas:

A The measurement of the cost of capital.

B The delineation and measurement of the effects of leverage.

C The establishment of an optimal capital structure.

D The establishment of the firm's proper financing policy.

II These four issues highlight the importance of environmental uncertainty.

A If a firm employs an all-equity capitalization, it is subject only to business risk.

B However, if a firm allows debt into its capitalization, it subjects itself to the additional burden of financial risk.

C Three types of income and expenditure streams are associated with business and financial risk:

1 Net operating income, NOI, which refers to the total cash earnings of the firm, after allowing for depreciation.

2 Net income, NI, which refers to the return to stockholders, after deducting for the interest charges on debt.

(a) Expected net income size varies directly with leverage or the debt-to-equity ratio of the firm, *ceteris paribus*.

(b) The quality (certainty) of anticipated net income varies inversely with leverage, *ceteris paribus*.

3 The annual interest cost of debt, C_d, can be expressed as the difference between NOI and NI.

D Three capitalization rates are associated with the firm's capital structure:

1 The debt capitalization rate, K_d, which is the effective yield to creditors on the firm's debt.

(a) The debt capitalization rate equals the annual interest costs of debt divided by the market value of outstanding debt.

(b) That is, $K_d = C_d/P_d$.

2 The equity capitalization rate, K_e, which is the effective yield to owners on the firm's equity.

(a) The equity capitalization rate equals the expected annual net income on equity divided by the market value of outstanding equity.
(b) That is, $K_e = NI/P_e$.

3 The overall capitalization rate, K_o, which is the effective yield to owners on the firm's total capital.
(a) The overall capitalization rate is the expected annual net operating income divided by the total market value of the firm.
(b) That is, $K_o = NOI/P_T$.

E These capitalization rates exhibit some interesting relationships.

1 They have a sequential relationship: $K_e > K_o > K_d$.
(a) $K_o > K_d$ accounts for the fact that the probability of obtaining the expected net operating income is less than the probability of achieving the minimum earnings necessary to pay the interest cost on debt.
(b) $K_e > K_o$ accounts for the fact that the probability of obtaining the expected net income is less than the probability of achieving the expected net operating income.

2 K_o is a weighted average of K_e and K_d:

$$K_o = X_1 K_e + X_2 K_d$$

where X_1 = proportion of equity to total market value of firm
X_2 = proportion of debt to total market value of firm
$X_1 + X_2 = 1$

III A criterion for the acceptance of investment proposals can be given in terms of the overall capitalization rate.

A Letting C equal the total cost of an investment proposal, accept the proposal if $\Delta\text{NOI}/C > K_o = X_1 K_e + X_2 K_d$.

B If one assumes a corporate income tax rate of T, then the above criterion becomes: Accept if $(1 - T)\,\Delta\text{NOI}/C > (1 - T)K_o$.

IV The weighted-average cost of capital is an average of the costs of each of the sources of funds used by the firm, weighted by the proportion that each holds in the firm's capital structure.

A One may use book-value weights or current market-value weights.

B Weighting schemes raise two interrelated questions:

1 Does the cost of raising funds remain invariant, or does it vary directly with the volume of funds raised?
2 Does the cost of raising funds remain invariant, or does it vary directly with the firm's capital structure?

V The above discussion on the combined cost of debt and equity has been facilitated by three artificial assumptions:

A The expected earnings from incremental investments are of the same quality as the earnings from the firm's existing assets.

B Corporate income taxes and the deductibility of interest payments do not affect the financial decisions of the firm.

C The firm's incremental investments are financed so that the capitalization of the firm retains the same proportion of debt to equity.

VI Since changes in leverage affect the quality of expected earnings, the capitalization rates will also change.

A If one assumes the firm's capitalization contains only pure debt and pure equity, leverage may be defined in one of three ways:

1 Leverage is the ratio of debt to equity, at market values; that is, $L = P_d/P_e$.
2 Leverage is the ratio of debt to total capital, at market values; that is, $L = P_d/(P_d + P_e)$.
3 Leverage is the ratio of debt costs to net operating income; that is, $L = C_d/\text{NOI}$.

B The following discussion of the effects of leverage on market capitalization rates will assume that leverage affects only K_o and K_e and will use the definition that $L = P_d/P_e$.

1 The net income approach capitalizes the net income of the firm at a constant equity capitalization rate, up to some very high rate of leverage.
 (a) Since K_o is a weighted average of K_e and K_d, as the degree of leverage increases the overall capitalization rate decreases toward K_d.
 (b) Within the relevant range, the total market value of the firm varies directly with leverage.
2 The net operating income approach capitalizes the net operating income of the firm at a constant overall capitalization rate, up to some very high rate of leverage.
 (a) Any increase in the firm's net income from the use of leverage is exactly offset by an equivalent decrease in the quality of earnings.
 (b) The total market value of the firm remains unchanged over the relevant range of capital structures.
3 The traditional approach suggests that the use of leverage only minimally affects the equity capitalization rate.
 (a) The increase in the equity capitalization rate does not entirely offset the increase in net earnings resulting from the use of low-cost debt.
 (b) Hence, for the firm that keeps its capital structure within the limits of capital-market acceptability, leverage is beneficial and increases the total market value of the firm.

VII There are some additional problems to be considered when measuring the combined cost of capital.

A Incremental investment proposals promise returns that are typically not of the same quality as those promised by the existing asset base.

B Incremental investment projects allow a different access to debt financing at different costs.

1 Hence, the use of a single K_o does not provide a uniform standard of comparison.
2 The specification of K_e in the acceptance criterion stated in III is one way of handling this problem since K_e accounts for the combination of business and financial risk.

C Corporate income taxes and the deductibility of interest and lease charges in the computation of tax liabilities present further analytical difficulties.

QUESTIONS FOR SELF-EXAMINATION

True or False

_____ 1 If a firm employs an all-debt capitalization, it is subject only to financial risk.

_____ 2 The quality of anticipated net income varies directly with leverage, *ceteris paribus*.

_____ 3 Because K_o is a weighted average of K_e and K_d, its value must lie between the values of K_e and K_d.

_____ 4 Leverage is the ratio of the firm's interest charges on debt to the equity of the firm.

_____ 5 The measurement of a firm's cost of capital is independent of its financing mix.

_____ 6 Net operating income refers to the total, after-depreciation cash earnings of a firm.

_____ 7 The annual interest cost of debt can be expressed as the difference between the cost of debt and the cost of equity.

_____ 8 K_e is the effective yield to owners on the firm's total capital.

_____ 9 According to the traditional approach to leverage, the total market value of the firm is increased through the use of leverage.

_____ 10 According to the investment criterion stated in this chapter, accept a proposal if $\Delta \text{NOI}/C > K_o$.

Multiple Choice

_____ 1 ________ refers to the return to stockholders, after deducting for the interest charges on debt.

(a) Net income
(b) The payout ratio
(c) Net operating income
(d) The overall capitalization rate

_____ 2 _____ is the effective yield to owners on the firm's equity.

(a) K_o
(b) K_e
(c) K_d
(d) NI

_____ 3 Given the following information, and assuming that all payments of interest and investment costs are made in one lump sum,

Interest rate = .10
Total debt = $80,000
Total equity = $320,000
Net operating income = $72,000

what is the value for the equity capitalization rate?

(a) .25
(b) .125
(c) .20
(d) .08

_____ 4 Assuming the same data as in question 3, what is the value of the debt capitalization rate?

(a) .125
(b) .06
(c) .10
(d) .15

_____ 5 In addition to the data in question 3, you are given the following information: A proposal costing $120,000 is expected to increase net operating income to $96,000 and leave the capitalization rates unchanged. Using the investment criterion stated in this chapter and ignoring taxes, should the proposal be accepted?

(a) Yes.
(b) No.
(c) It does not matter.

PROBLEMS FOR PRACTICE

1 Two firms, A and B, have equal earnings before interest and taxes of $160,000 with an associated standard deviation of $12,000. However, Firm A has a debt-asset ratio of 0% and Firm B

has a 25% debt-asset ratio. The total market value for each firm is $4 million, and their average interest cost of debt is 6%. Calculate the coefficient of variation of net income for each firm. (a) Ignore income taxes. (b) Include a marginal corporate tax rate of 40%.

Solution

When observations are linearly transformed, the following relationship is maintained: If $y = a + bx$, then $\sigma_y = |b|\sigma_x$.

(a) Interest on debt for Firm B:

$4,000,000 × .25 × .06 = $60,000

	Firm A	*Firm B*
EBIT	$160,000	$160,000
Interest	—	60,000
Net income	$160,000	$100,000
$CV = \dfrac{\sigma}{NI}$	$\dfrac{\$\ 12{,}000}{\$160{,}000} = .075$	$\dfrac{\$\ 12{,}000}{\$100{,}000} = .12$

(b)

	Firm A	*Firm B*
EBIT	$160,000	$160,000
Interest	—	60,000
Taxable income	$160,000	$100,000
Taxes (40%)	64,000	40,000
Net income	$ 96,000	$ 60,000

$$CV = \frac{(1 - T)\sigma}{NI} \qquad \frac{(.6)(12{,}000)}{96{,}000} = .075 \qquad \frac{(.6)(12{,}000)}{60{,}000} = .12$$

2 The Equip Company has 300,000 outstanding shares of common stock. Its expected earnings per share are $2.75, and based on these expected earnings, the common stock is selling at a *P/E* ratio of 8. The company also has an outstanding bond issue with a par value of $3,200,000 and a coupon rate of 5%. According to its market values, the company possesses a 40% debt-equity ratio. Determine the (a) equity-, (b) debt-, and (c) overall-capitalization rates for Equip Company. (Ignore corporate income taxes.)

Solution

(a) Equity-capitalization rate, K_e

300,000 shares × $2.75 = $825,000 net income, NI

$2.75 × 8 × 300,000 shares = $6,600,000 market value of equity, P_e

$$K_e = \frac{NI}{P_e} = \frac{\$825{,}000}{\$6{,}600{,}000} = .125 = 12.5\%$$

(b) Debt-capitalization rate, K_d

.40 × $6,600,000 = $2,640,000 market value of debt, P_d

.05 × $3,200,000 = $160,000 interests costs on debt, C_d

$$K_d = \frac{C_d}{P_d} = \frac{\$160{,}000}{\$2{,}640{,}000} = .0606 = 6.06\%$$

(c) Overall capitalization rate, K_o

$$X_1 = \frac{\$6{,}600{,}000}{\$6{,}600{,}000 + \$2{,}640{,}000} = .714$$

$X_2 = 1 - X_1 = 1 - .714 = .286$

$K_o = K_e X_1 + K_d X_2 = (12.5)(.714) + (6.06)(.286) = 10.66\%$

3 The current balance sheet of High, Inc. appears in part as follows:

Balance Sheet (12/31/74)

Mortgage bonds, 3%, due 1984	$ 1,000,000
Debentures, 5%, due 1989	3,000,000
Preferred stock, 5,000 shares, 4% div.	500,000
Common stock, 1,000,000 shares	1,000,000
Retained earnings	9,000,000
	$14,500,000

Current market data for High, Inc.

Market value of mortgage bond	$664
Market value of debenture	$743
Market value of share of preferred stock	$ 67
Market value of share of common stock	$ 35

Compute the book-value weights and the market-value weights for each component of the capital structure of High, Inc.

Solution

Book-value Weights:

	(In thousands)		*Weights (%)*
Mortgage bonds	$\frac{1,000}{14,500}$	=	6.9
Debentures	$\frac{3,000}{14,500}$	=	20.7
Preferred stock	$\frac{500}{14,500}$	=	3.4
Common stock	$\frac{1,000}{14,500}$	=	6.9
Retained earnings	$\frac{9,000}{14,500}$	=	62.1
			100.0%

Market-value Weights:

		Market Values	*Weights (%)*
Mortgage bonds	(1,000,000/1,000) × $664 =	$ 664,000	1.7
Debentures	(3,000,000/1,000) × $743 =	2,229,000	5.8
Preferred stock	5,000 × $ 67 =	335,000	.9
Common stock	1,000,000 × $ 35 =	35,000,000	91.6
		$38,228,000	100.0%

4 High, Inc. has the opportunity to invest in projects returning 16%. Currently they are paying a $1.75 dividend per share of common stock from earnings of $3.90 per share. Their marginal corporate tax rate is 40%. The market yield on their bonds and debentures is 8%. Based on this data and information obtained in Problem 3, determine the market-weighted average cost of capital.

Solution

Effective cost of bonds and debentures:

$8\%(1 - T) = 8\%(1 - .40) = 4.8\%$

Effective cost of preferred stock:

$$\frac{\text{Dividend}}{\text{Market value}} = \frac{\$100 \times .04}{\$67} = .0597 = 5.97\%$$

Effective cost of common stock:

$$b = \text{retention rate} = 1 - \frac{\$1.75}{\$3.90} = .551$$

$$K_e = \frac{D}{P} + br = \frac{1.75}{35} + (.551)(.16) = .138 = 13.8\%$$

	Market Weights	*Effective Cost (%)*	*Weighted Cost (%)*
Mortgage bonds	.017	4.80	.082
Debentures	.058	4.80	.278
Preferred stock	.009	5.97	.054
Common stock	.916	13.80	12.641
	1.000		13.055%

PROBLEMS FOR SELF-EXAMINATION

5 Company *X* is planning to invest $900,000 in a project with an expected return of 18%. The necessary funds are to be obtained from retained earnings, new common stock, and new debentures. The company considers the current capital structure based on market values as optimal. The following data apply to the current position of the company:

Common stock: 100,000 shares outstanding with a dividend per share of $1.20 representing a payout ratio of 40%. Current *P/E* is 14. New issues require a 10% flotation cost.

Debentures: $1,000 par value per bond with a total book value of $2.5 million. The current market value per bond is $920 yielding 7.5%.

The marginal tax rate is 40%. Calculate the market-weighted average cost of capital for the new funds.

Solution

9 Capital Structure and Optimal Financial Policy

Theme Chapter 9 outlines the three major views on capital structure, a central and permeating issue of the financial management program.

I Capital structure has many relevant dimensions.

A The capital structure of the firm involves the following topics:

1 The financing mix.
2 Investment decisions.
3 The optimal use of leverage.
4 The timing of investment and financing transactions.
5 Acceptable levels of risk and liquidity.

B Capital structure may be dealt with at three different levels of complexity:

1 The existence of an optimal asset structure is a static proposition that requires a unique solution for the cost of capital.
(a) Management should obtain the mix of financial claims that minimizes the cost of capital.
(b) Capital structure is, therefore, regarded as the active policy variable.
2 Capital structure is a comparative static proposition that yields different values for the cost of capital and the capital structure as the underlying parameters change.
3 Capital structure is a dynamic process of interdependent investment and financing decisions, the by-product of the continual process of matching uses and sources of funds.

C An optimal capital structure is that combination of debt and equity which attains the stated goals of management, heretofore assumed to be the maximization of market value and the implied minimization of the cost of capital.

D The three major views on capital structure are the traditional approach, the Modigliani and Miller view, and the intermediate net operating income approach.

II The traditional approach suggests that the market value of the firm will, *ceteris paribus*, rise for small values of leverage, remain nearly constant through intermediate values, and decline for high leverage values.

A The rationale of this approach is its proponents' belief that the market reacts to leverage in three distinct stages:

1 As the firm begins to use leverage, the use of low-cost debt causes net income to increase faster than the corresponding increase in K_e and causes the annual interest cost on debt to rise faster than the corresponding rise in K_d.

(a) Hence, the market value of the firm will increase according to the equation $P_T = NI/K_e + C_d/K_d$.
(b) Furthermore, since a portion of the firm's assets is financed with debt at a lower cost than the cost of equity, K_o will decrease according to the equation $K_o = X_1 K_e + X_2 K_d$.

2 Once the firm has achieved a certain degree of leverage, moderate additions of debt to its capital structure do not affect its market value or its overall cost of capital.
(a) Increases in net income are offset by increases in K_e and K_d.
(b) Hence, the total market value of the firm remains constant.

3 Beyond a critical value of leverage, further additions of debt to the firm's capital structure result in a falling market value and a rising overall cost of capital.

III The Modigliani and Miller view, hereafter abbreviated as the MM argument, is that in the absence of corporate income taxes, market value and the cost of capital are independent of the leverage of the firm.

A The irrelevance of leverage derives from the hypothesis that, irrespective of the effects of leverage on interest rates, K_e will rise by an amount sufficient to offset any possible savings from the use of low-cost debt.

B MM argue that in a world of perfect markets and rational investors, two firms promising net operating incomes of the same size and quality cannot have different market values.

1 This argument is not surprising, though, since it is tautologically true.
2 Should a discrepancy in market values occur, MM propose a simple switching mechanism, loosely called arbitrage, which enables investors to engage in personal leverage, realize a net gain, and, resultantly, restore price equilibrium in the market.

C The three MM propositions are

1 Proposition I: The market value of the firm is independent of the degree of leverage and is found by capitalizing the expected normal net operating income, $\overline{NOI}$, at the overall cost of capital; that is, $P_T = \overline{NOI}/K_o$.
2 Proposition II: The cost of common equity is equal to the constant average cost of capital plus an adjustment for financial risk; that is, $K_e = K_o + (K_o - K_d) P_d/P_e$.
3 Proposition III: The cutoff point for investments will always be K_o; that is, accept a proposal if it promises a rate of return greater than the overall cost of capital.

D Stated are some additional assumptions of the MM view:

1 Corporations can be empirically grouped into homogeneous risk classes.
2 The expected net operating income of the firm is a random variable.
3 All current and potential investors have arrived at the same estimate of the expected normal net operating income.

E Criticism of the MM argument centers on the switching mechanism.

1 Little attention is paid to corporate income taxes and the deductibility of interest payments.
2 The simple arbitrage model assumes away the possible differences between corporate and personal leverage.
(a) Given the greater credit-worthiness of corporations, their borrowing rates are normally lower than those for individuals.
(b) Given the possibility of default and margin calls, there may be less risk in corporate than in individual borrowing.
(c) The cost of personal borrowing is normally invariant with respect to leverage.
3 Transactions costs and capital-gains taxes might reduce the effectiveness of the arbitrage mechanism.
4 No allowance is made for the risk of bankruptcy.

IV The net operating income view argues that changes in the capital structure of the firm do not change the firm's overall risk content.

A The capital structure change merely redistributes the risk among the holders of the financial claims on the firm.

B Hence, there is not a leverage effect.

C Because of the tax treatment of debt and market imperfections, though, the judicious combination of financial claims can lead to an optimal capital structure.

V A few more considerations of the financing decision now appear:

A The stability of net operating earnings conditions the degree of allowable leverage.

B The leverage decision should also take into account the time factors of the various debt claims, e.g., the duration of the claim, the timing of interest payments, and renewals.

C The amount of external financing may affect the cost of capital through factor indivisibility or factor scarcity.

1 Factor indivisibility is the inverse relationship between the per dollar cost of raising new, external capital and the amount raised.
2 Factor scarcity relates the size and influence of the firm to the credit market.

QUESTIONS FOR SELF-EXAMINATION

True or False

____ 1 The static level of complexity regards capital structure as the active policy variable.

____ 2 The dynamic level of complexity regards capital structure as a by-product of the economic system in which the firm operates.

____ 3 The proponents of the traditional approach to capital structure view the market as being indifferent to leverage.

____ 4 Given their assumptions, Modigliani and Miller argue that market value and the cost of capital are independent of the firm's leverage.

____ 5 If a discrepancy in market values occurs, MM argue that, *ceteris paribus*, the overall capitalization rate for the undervalued firm will fall and, resultantly, restore price stability in the market.

____ 6 MM propose the acceptance of a project if it promises a rate of return greater than the overall cost of capital.

____ 7 Criticism of the MM argument has centered on the difficulty of grouping corporations into homogeneous risk classes.

____ 8 The net operating income view does not admit a leverage effect.

____ 9 Because changes in capital structure merely redistribute risk according to the net operating income view, an optimal capital structure cannot exist.

____ 10 The per dollar cost of raising new, external capital is inversely related to the amount raised.

Multiple Choice

____ 1, ____ 2 Whereas the firm's capital structure according to the static level of complexity requires ____ for the cost of capital, the comparative static proposition yields ____ for the cost of capital.

(a) different values
(b) equal values
(c) a unique value
(d) similar values

____ 3 According to the traditional view, once the firm has achieved some intermediate degree of leverage, moderate additions of debt to its capital structure ______ its market value.
(a) do not change
(b) increase
(c) change by an indeterminate amount
(d) decrease

____ 4 The MM argument for the irrelevance of leverage is derived from the ______
(a) arbitrage argument.
(b) assumed rise in K_e to offset any advantageous use of low-cost debt.
(c) hypothesized reaction of the market to leverage.
(d) capitalization of the expected normal capital gain.

____ 5 The MM argument is criticized because of its treatment of ____
(a) bankruptcy.
(b) transactions costs.
(c) corporate versus personal leverage.
(d) all the above.

PROBLEMS FOR PRACTICE

1 Fore Company has expected net operating income of \$500,000 and interest costs of \$20,000. Its equity and debt capitalization rates are 10% and 5%, respectively. Assume no corporation income taxes. Determine the market value of the firm and its overall average cost of capital.

Solution

\$500,000 − \$20,000 = \$480,000 net income, NI

$$P_T = \frac{NI}{K_e} + \frac{C_d}{K_d} = \frac{\$480{,}000}{.10} + \frac{\$20{,}000}{.05} = \$4{,}800{,}000 + \$400{,}000 = \$5{,}200{,}000$$

$$K_o = \frac{NOI}{P_T} = \frac{\$500{,}000}{\$5{,}200{,}000} = 9.615\%$$

2 Subsequently, the interest costs of Fore Company double because of additional debt incurred; however, its net operating income remains constant. The increased debt-equity ratio results in an equity capitalization rate of 10.2%. Continuing the assumption of no corporate income taxes, what is the market value and overall capitalization rate for the firm? Is the company operating in a world hypothesized by Modigliani and Miller or by the traditionalists?

Solution

\$500,000 − \$40,000 = \$460,000 net income, NI

$$P_T = \frac{\$460{,}000}{.102} + \frac{\$40{,}000}{.05} = \$4{,}509{,}804 + \$800{,}000 = \$5{,}309{,}804$$

$$K_o = \frac{\$500{,}000}{\$5{,}309{,}804} = 9.417\%$$

The market value of the firm, P_T, has increased, and the overall average cost of capital, K_o, has decreased with the judicious use of debt capital. Thus the company is operating in a world as viewed by the traditionalists.

3 If the Fore Company in Problems 1 and 2 exists in the Modigliani-Miller world, what is its

(a) market value, (b) overall cost of capital, and (c) cost-of-equity capital given the increase in debt capital of Problem 2?

Solution

(a) Market value, P_T = \$5,200,000 (no change)

(b) Overall cost of capital, K_o = 9.615% (no change)

(c) Cost-of-equity capital, K_e:

$$P_d = \frac{C_d}{K_d} = \frac{\$40{,}000}{.05} = \$800{,}000$$

$$P_e = P_T - P_d = \$5{,}200{,}000 - \$800{,}000 = \$4{,}400{,}000$$

$$K_e = K_o + (K_o - K_d)\frac{P_d}{P_e} = 9.615 + (9.615 - 5.0)\frac{800{,}000}{4{,}400{,}000}$$

$$= 9.615 + .839 = 10.454\%$$

Alternatively,

$$K_e = \frac{\text{NI}}{P_e} = \frac{\$460{,}000}{\$4{,}400{,}000} = 10.454\%$$

PROBLEMS FOR SELF-EXAMINATION

4 The Ding Company earns \$100,000 expected net operating income on total assets. The total assets have a market value of \$1 million. Their schedule of the cost-of-debt capital at different levels of debt-to-total assets is as follows:

Debt-asset Ratio	K_d
0	5%
10%	5%
20%	5%
30%	6%

In a Modigliani-Miller framework with no corporate income taxes and assuming a constant level of net operating income and total assets, calculate the cost-of-equity capital for the above debt-asset ratios.

Solution

10 Empirical Tests of the Modigliani-Miller Cost-of-Capital Hypothesis

Theme Chapter 10 reviews a series of empirical studies that were specifically designed to test Modigliani and Miller's Propositions I and II.

I Restatement of Propositions I and II.

A Proposition I: The market value of the firm is independent of the degree of leverage and is computed by capitalizing the expected normalized net operating income at the average cost of capital; that is, $P_T = \overline{NOI}/K_o$.

1 Assuming a sample of homogeneous firms, a regression of the average cost of capital, $\overline{NOI}/P_T$, on the capital structure, P_d/P_T, would be expected to produce a horizontal or nearly horizontal line.

2 However, if the regression results in a U-shaped curve, indicating the relative advantage of debt within a market-acceptable range, then the traditional view of capital structure would tend to be verified.

B Proposition II: The cost of common equity is equal to the constant average cost of capital plus an adjustment for financial risk; that is, $K_e = K_o + (K_o - K_d)P_d/P_e$.

1 Hence, one would expect a straight line with a positive slope to result from a regression of K_e on P_d/P_e.

2 However, if the regression results in an upside-down, U-shaped curve, indicating the relative disadvantage of debt beyond the market-acceptable debt-to-equity ratio, then the traditional view would tend to be verified.

II Modigliani and Miller: first study.

A Their original study used a sample of 43 electric utilities from 1947 and 1948, a sample of 42 oil companies from 1953, and essentially the same analytical framework as that stated in I above.

B Because the test of Proposition I resulted in regression equations with slopes nearly equal to zero, i.e., the regression equations were almost horizontal lines, their first proposition was supported empirically.

C Because the test of Proposition II resulted in correlation coefficients for the two variables that were positive and significantly different from zero, their second proposition was also supported empirically.

D A number of objections, though, have been raised against the methodology of Modigliani and Miller and, therefore, their results.

1 There was a lack of observations for the electric utilities in the low- and high-leverage ranges.

2 There was a high degree of heterogeneity among the firms in the samples.
3 In the test of Proposition I, the inclusion of P_T in the denominator of both the independent and dependent variable tended to increase the degree of correlation and introduced a positive bias in the slopes of the regression equations.
4 The tests failed to account for the growth rate and size of the firms.

III Barges study.

A The study was meticulously designed to improve upon the limitations of the first MM study.

1 Barges used the railroad, cement, and department store industries for the year 1956 to reveal homogeneous stability, growth, and recovery, respectively.
2 He rejected as biased the measures used by MM and regressed the average cost of capital on the book-value debt-to-equity ratio.

B The tests using the railroad industry were inconclusive for Proposition II and refuted Proposition I; the tests using the cement and department store industries refuted Proposition II, but were not conducted for Proposition I.

IV Weston study.

A Weston attempted to improve on MM's original study by specifying the aftertax average cost of capital as a function of the debt ratio (P_d/P_T), total assets, and per share earnings growth. He used data from 59 electric utilities for the year 1959.

B The resultant regression equation implied an inverse relationship between the average cost of capital and the leverage ratio; this result is congruent with both the MM argument and the traditional view, though, because leverage is an inverse function of per share earnings growth.

C He also attempted to clarify some measurement problems by testing three different measures of the cost of capital.

V Modigliani and Miller: second study.

A The second study on Propositions I and II attempted primarily to find trends in the cost-of-capital variable.

B MM used a sample of 63 electric utilities from 1954, 1956, and 1957 and attempted to rectify some of the shortcomings of their first study.

C Again MM concluded that their study supported the original hypotheses, and once more their methodology and results were criticized.

VI Other studies.

A Wippern tested for the validity of Proposition II, but with a more representative data base and by redefining leverage as the ratio of fixed charges to cash flow properly adjusted for downside risk. He tested data from seven industries for the years 1956, 1958, 1961, and 1963.

1 His 10-variable, multiple-regression model accounted for such factors as leverage, growth, payout, and firm size.
2 Wippern concluded that his test supported the traditional view since the cost-of-equity capital varied directly with the leverage.

B The Sarma and Rao study was conducted in the developing economy of India. It investigated the engineering industry for the years 1962, 1964, and 1965. They computed coefficients that supported the prudent use of leverage, thus supporting the traditional view.

QUESTIONS FOR SELF-EXAMINATION

Multiple Choice

_____ 1 Regression analysis attempting to verify Proposition I would be expected to produce _______

(a) a U-shaped curve.
(b) an upside-down, U-shaped curve.
(c) a positively sloped, straight line.
(d) a horizontal line.

_____ 2 Regression analysis attempting to verify Proposition II would be expected to produce _______

(a) a U-shaped curve.
(b) a polynomial.
(c) a positively sloped, straight line.
(d) none of the above.

_____ 3 Which of the following is not a criticism of Modigliani and Miller's first study?

(a) Observations for one of the samples did not include low- and high-leverage values.
(b) The samples possessed a serious degree of homogeneity.
(c) The tests failed to account for the growth rate and size of the firms.
(d) None of the above.

_____ 4 The Barges study explicitly improved upon what two criticisms of the first MM study?

(a) Insufficient leverage observations and the heterogeneity of samples
(b) The failure to account for growth rates and insufficient leverage observations
(c) The biased slopes of the regression equations and the heterogeneity of samples
(d) The failure to account for the size of firms and the biased slopes of the regression equations

_____ 5 Weston attempted to improve on MM's original study by specifying the aftertax average cost of capital as a function of the debt ratio, total assets, and _______

(a) payout.
(b) per share earnings growth.
(c) an industry classification.
(d) the interest rate.

_____ 6 MM's second study _____ reliable evidence in support of Propositions I and II.

(a) failed to give
(b) provided
(c) tended to give
(d) obscured

_____ 7 Wippern attempted to reach relevant conclusions by obtaining a more representative data base and by _______

(a) redefining the measure for leverage.
(b) working with data from a developing economy.
(c) isolating homogeneous firms.
(d) testing different measures of the cost of capital.

APPENDIX

A Corporate Dividend Policies

Theme The effect of dividend policy on market valuation is one of the most controversial issues of finance. Empirical studies on corporate dividend policies have attempted to clarify this issue.

I Dividend policy and valuation.

A John B. Williams has defined the market value of a financial asset as the present value of all the estimated future dividends, properly discounted for futurity, and the alternatives available to the investor.

B However, a number of problems are associated with Williams' work because it is based primarily on the maximization of income to the firm.

C The various attempts to link functionally the dividend policy of the firm with market valuation can be classified into three hypotheses:

1 The passive residual hypothesis, which is formulated in terms of the magnitudes of the marginal rate of return from proposed investments and the market capitalization rate.
(a) If the former is larger than the latter, the firm should reinvest all its earnings; if the converse is true, the firm should distribute as dividends all its earnings.
(b) The equality of the two rates would imply indifference between reinvestment and payout.

2 The irrelevance of dividends hypothesis, first proposed by Modigliani and Miller, states that the investment decisions of the firm are independent of its dividend policy.
(a) Hence, the present and future dividends of the firm are irrelevant to the market valuation of its earnings.
(b) This conclusion is based on the three following assumptions:
i Perfect capital markets
ii Investor indifference between capital gains and dividends
iii Complete certainty about future corporate investments and profits

3 The dividend effect hypothesis posits a direct relationship between the dividend policies of the firm and the market valuation of its earnings.
(a) It is derived from the second principle of the rational investor.
(b) Specifically, this hypothesis assumes that investors generally exhibit risk-averse behavior and associate future returns with a higher risk factor than present returns.

D Modigliani and Miller, however, have admitted to three situations where a change in the dividend rate may affect security prices:

1 For firms with long-established and generally appreciated policies of stable adjustments to target payout ratios, any change in the dividend rate may possess informational

content; i.e., a change might be interpreted as an announcement of a revision of management's expectation of future profits.

2 Such firms, as described above, may reflect a clientele effect; i.e., they may attract investors whose preferred time pattern and stability coincide with the firm's dividend policy.

3 In the short run, it is possible that a firm might exploit the informational content of dividends to affect a change in its market price.

II Empirical studies on corporate dividend policies.

A One of the earliest and most controversial studies was conducted by John Lintner.

1 He proposed and verified the hypothesis that management directs its policies toward the stabilization of the dividend rate.

2 His hypothesis assumes that managers believe stockholders place a premium on securities which yield stable dividends.

B However, subsequent research has not substantiated unequivocally Lintner's conclusion.

1 Bicksler's study concluded that there was no statistically significant relationship between the target payout ratio derived from Lintner's model and the share price of a firm determined by two valuation models.

2 Ezzell's study concluded that there is a direct empirical relationship between dividend rate instability and market share prices.

3 In two older and related empirical studies, similar results have occurred.

(a) Darling concluded that companies will adjust their dividends to new earnings gradually and in line with a stabilization policy.

(b) Brittain concluded that the actual dividend is gradually adjusted in line with the target payout ratio.

QUESTIONS FOR SELF-EXAMINATION

True or False

_____ 1 The passive residual hypothesis treats dividends as the by-product of the investment decisions of the firm.

_____ 2 The clientele effect refers to the attraction of investors to those firms that pay dividends which correspond to their time pattern and stability preferences.

_____ 3 All empirical studies on corporate dividend policies conclude or imply that investors place a premium on securities which yield stable dividends.

_____ 4 The irrelevance of dividends hypothesis and the dividend effect hypothesis are opposite positions to the same issue but may be compatible in certain situations.

_____ 5 The informational content of dividends refers to how a change in the historically established rate of dividend payment may cause a change in the expectations of stockholders.

APPENDIX

B Specialized Investment Decisions: Lease Financing

Theme Appendix B considers the benefits and costs of lease financing for investment projects as an alternative to debt or equity financing.

I A financial lease is considerably different from an operating lease.

A In a financial lease, the lessee enters into an irrevocable, legal obligation to make a series of payments, over a long contractual horizon, to the lessor, in exchange for the use of a productive asset.

B In an operating lease, a rental fee entitles the lessee to the use of an asset over a short or intermediate, contractual horizon; an operating lease is usually terminable on relatively short notice.

II Some typical attributes of financial leases are

A The lessor retains the title to the leased asset but surrenders the economic value of the asset to the lessee.

B The contractual horizon of the financial lease typically coincides with the economic life of the leased asset.

C The total payment due the lessor exceeds the purchase price of the asset because it includes his return on investment.

D The terms and obligations of the financial lease are delineated in a contract that, at the very least, must contain the following items:

1 The time period during which the contract is irrevocable.
2 The amount and timing of the periodic payments to the lessor.
3 The renewal or purchase options.
4 The arrangement for maintenance, insurance, and other expenses.

III Basically, there are two types of financial leasing arrangements:

A Direct leasing, which involves the lease of an asset by its manufacturer or an intermediary, such as a leasing company, finance company, or bank.

B The sale and leaseback arrangement, which involves the sale of an asset by its ultimate user to another party and the subsequent lease of it back to the original owner and ultimate user.

IV Some considerations included in the decision to lease an asset or finance it through debt appear below.

A Advantages of lease financing:

1 It provides economic flexibility, particularly with the type of production equipment that is subject to a high rate of obsolescence.
2 It lacks some of the protective covenants that are typically used in debt financing.
3 It provides 100% financing, as opposed to less than 100% financing when debt is employed.
4 In the case of bankruptcy or reorganization, a lessor is entitled to only one year's rent, whereas a lender is entitled to three years' rent.
5 It has some possible tax advantages, particularly in the case of leasing land, since the cost of the land is amortized in the lease payments.
6 Lease obligations appear only as a footnote to the firm's audited financial statements.

B Limitations of lease financing:

1 The value of the asset, particularly real estate, may increase during the lease period, depriving the lessee of a potential capital gain.
2 The interest cost of lease financing is generally higher than that of debt financing.
3 The higher fixed charges and 100% financing of a lease increase the financial risk of the firm.

V The decision to lease the services of a productive asset or to finance it by contracting debt can be made with either of the following two criteria:

A The discounted cash-flow (DCF) technique compares the present value of the expenditures associated with leasing and borrowing.

1 The present value of the leasing costs is computed as follows:

$$PV_L = \sum_{t=1}^{n} L_t(1 - T)/(1 + r)^t$$

where n = number years in lease contract
L_t = uniform lease payment at end of each year, t
T = marginal tax rate on corporate net income
r = firm's rate of return on incremental investment

2 The present value of the borrowing costs is computed as follows:

$$PV_B = \sum_{t=1}^{n} [B_t + i_t - (i_t + D_t)T]/(1 + r)^t + P_o$$

where B_t = uniform principle payment
i_t = debt charge at end of year, t
D_t = depreciation charge on asset for year t
P_o = down payment

3 The DCF acceptance criterion is stated below.
(a) If $PV_L < PV_B$, lease the asset.
(b) If $PV_L > PV_B$, borrow to finance the asset.
(c) If $PV_L = PV_B$, use either type of financing.
4 The DCF technique has a few shortcomings.
(a) The tax-savings effects are confounded with the amount of funds available under the two options.
(b) The larger amount of financing provided under the lease option will increase the financial risk of the firm and, hence, the discount rate of the firm.
(c) The different rates of discount are not accounted for in DCF analysis.

B The basic interest rate (BIR) approach isolates the tax effect and accounts for the difference in the amounts of financing.

1 The discounted cost of leasing is equal to

$$C - \sum_{t=1}^{n} (L_t - kP_t)T/(1 + r)^t$$

where C = cash price of the asset
k = cost of borrowing from equipment supplier
P_t = amount of debt outstanding during year t

2 The discounted cost of borrowing is equal to

$$C - \sum_{t=1}^{n} D_t T/(1 + r)^t$$

3 The BIR acceptance criterion requires that the decision maker choose the alternative with the smaller of the two costs.

VI There are two other ways to evaluate the lease- and debt-financing options:

A The effective yield analysis of loan equivalents bypasses present values in favor of the effective interest cost, and assumes that the repayment schedules of the two options have the same configuration.

B Another method evaluates the two options by separating the cash flows associated with financing from the cash flows associated with tax savings. This approach also assumes equivalent repayment schedules.

QUESTIONS FOR SELF-EXAMINATION

True or False

_____ 1 The essential differences between a financial lease and an operating lease are the irrevocable contract and longer contractual horizon of the former arrangement.

_____ 2 The desirability of lease financing derives from the fact that the total payment due the lessor is less than the purchase price of the asset.

_____ 3 Because the contractual horizon of the financial lease typically coincides with the economic life of the leased asset, the lessee has, in effect, made an outright purchase with 100% financing.

_____ 4 In the case of bankruptcy or reorganization, the firm faces a smaller liability with a leasing arrangement than with debt financing.

_____ 5 The 100% financing of a lease decreases the financial risk of the firm.

_____ 6 The different amounts of financing provided by the lease and debt options create the illusion that leasing is cheaper than borrowing.

_____ 7 One of the shortcomings of DCF analysis is its failure to account for the different discount rates of lease and debt financing.

_____ 8 Direct leasing involves the lease of an asset by its manufacturer or an intermediary.

Multiple Choice

_____ 1 Which of the following is not an advantage of lease financing?
(a) It lacks some protective covenants.
(b) It has some possible tax advantages.
(c) Lease obligations appear on financial statements as footnotes.
(d) The value of the leased asset may increase during the lease period.

_____ 2 Which of the following methods avoids the difficult choice of a discount rate?
(a) The basic interest rate approach
(b) The effective yield analysis of loan equivalents

(c) The discounted benefit-cost ratio
(d) The discounted cash-flow technique

_____ _____ 3 For which two shortcomings of the DCF technique does the BIR approach account explicitly?

(a) The tax effect
(b) The different discount rates
(c) The different amounts of financing
(d) Economic uncertainty

PROBLEMS FOR PRACTICE

1 The Scrap Company is going to install a new $20,000 baling machine at one of their branch stations. They have the opportunity to lease it for $4,800 per year or to borrow funds from their banker at 8% interest. If they borrow to purchase the baler, a 10% down payment is required with the principal amount due at the end of the fifth year. The life of the machine is five years and has nominal salvage value. They use straight-line depreciation. Their cost of capital is 12%, and their marginal tax rate if 40%. Employing the discounted cash-flow method, should Scrap Company lease or purchase the machine?

Solution

Leasing:

$L_t(1 - T) = \$4{,}800(1 - .4) = 4{,}800 \times .06 = \$2{,}880/\text{year}$

PV of $1 annually for 5 years at 12% = 3.605

$PV_L = \$2{,}880 \times 3.605 = \$10{,}382$

Borrow and purchase:

Depreciation = $20,000/5 years = $4,000/year

Down payment = P_o = $20,000 × .10 = $2,000

Amount borrowed = $20,000 − $2,000 = $18,000

Interest = i_t = $18,000 × .08 = $1,440/year

Year	i_t	B_t	D_t	$i_t + D_t$	$(i_t + D_t)T$	$B_t + i_t - (i_t + D_t)T$
1	$1,440	$ 0	$4,000	$5,440	$2,176	$ −736
2	1,440	0	4,000	5,440	2,176	−736
3	1,440	0	4,000	5,440	2,176	−736
4	1,440	0	4,000	5,440	2,176	−736
5	1,440	18,000	4,000	5,440	2,176	17,264

PV: $ −736 × 3.037 = $−2,235
17,264 × .567 = 9,789
$ 7,554

$PV_B = \$7{,}554 + \$2{,}000 = \$9{,}554$

Since $PV_B < PV_L$, purchase the machine with borrowed funds.

2 Because of the results from Problem 1, Scrap Company has decided to borrow the necessary funds and purchase the baling machine. However, the bank has changed the terms of the loan. A 10% down payment is still required, but the principal must be paid back in five installments with an 8% interest rate on the unpaid balance. The annual payments of principal plus interest are identical for all five years. Will this change the decision of Scrap Company to purchase rather than lease the machine?

Solution

Leasing:

PV_L = \$10,382 (no change)

Borrow and purchase:

Annual loan payment: PV of \$1 annually for 5 years at 8% = 3.993

$\frac{\$18,000}{3.993}$ = \$4,508 annual payment.

Interest for first year = \$18,000 × .08 = \$1,440

Year	$B_t + i_t$	i_t	B_t	Unpaid Balance	D_t
1	\$4,508	\$1,440	\$3,068	\$14,932	\$4,000
2	4,508	1,195	3,313	11,619	4,000
3	4,508	929	3,579	8,040	4,000
4	4,508	643	3,865	4,175	4,000
5	4,508	333	4,175	0	4,000

Year	$i_t + D_t$	$(i_t + D_t)T$	$B_t + i_t - (i_t + D_t)T$	PV of \$1 at 12%	PV
1	\$5,440	\$2,176	\$2,332	.893	\$2,082
2	5,195	2,078	2,430	.797	1,937
3	4,930	1,972	2,536	.712	1,806
4	4,643	1,857	2,651	.636	1,686
5	4,334	1,734	2,774	.567	1,573
					\$9,084

PV_B = \$9,084 + \$2,000 = \$11,084

Now $PV_B > PV_L$; thus, decision is to lease the baling machine.

3 The Scrap Company has decided to change methods for analyzing lease arrangements. Given the information in Problem 1, analyze the lease and borrow-purchase alternatives by the basic interest rate (BIR) method. Which alternative is preferred?

Solution

Discounted cost of borrowing-purchase (DCB):

D_t = \$4,000/year

D_tT = \$4,000 × .4 = \$1,600/year

PV of \$1 annually for 5 years at 12% = 3.605

PV = \$1,600 × 3.605 = \$5,768

DCB = \$20,000 − \$5,768 = \$14,232

Discounted cost of leasing (DCL):

L_t = \$4,800 P_t = \$18,000

kP_t = .08 × \$18,000 = \$1,440

$L_t - kP_t$ = \$4,800 − \$1,440 = \$3,360

$(L_t - kP_t)T$ = \$3,360 × .4 = \$1,344

PV = \$1,344 × 3.605 = \$4,845

DCL = \$20,000 − \$4,845 = \$15,155

Since DCB < DCL, the baling machine should be purchased with borrowed funds.

PROBLEMS FOR SELF-EXAMINATION

4 The business of Wholesale Distributing Company has grown considerably over the past year. To accommodate the increased business, their fleet of trucks must be expanded. They can lease three trucks from Overall Rentals for six years at a cost of $4,400 per year. Doe Trucks will sell them three trucks at $8,000 each with an agreement to repurchase the trucks at the end of the six years for $500 each. The bank will loan Wholesale 85% of the value of the trucks at 10% interest, payable on the unpaid balance. The loan is to be repaid in six equal annual installments. Wholesale depreciates assets by the straight-line method. Their cost of capital is 12%, and their marginal tax rate is 40%. What is the recommended financing alternative if the discounted cash-flow method is the technique for analysis?

Solution

5 Joseph Flory is debating whether to lease or buy a new car. Since it will be his business car, he will depreciate it over two years using straight-line depreciation. The car will cost $4,000 to purchase, and he expects to sell it for $1,000 at the end of two years. The dealer will finance it at 8% interest; however, Joe anticipates a 16% return on investment in the car. Joe also has the opportunity to lease the same model car from another dealer for $2,000 per year. Joe's marginal tax rate is 36%. Do you advise him to lease or buy the car, based on the basic interest rate approach? 73

Solution

11 Short-Term Uses of Funds

Theme The discussion in Chapter 11 is on three important, short-term uses of funds: cash and marketable securities, accounts receivable, and inventories.

I The level of working capital typically involves a marginal trade off between profitability and risk.

A Generally, short-term uses of funds are less risky and less profitable than long-term uses.

B Short-term sources of funds adjust more flexibly to seasonal fluctuations and are less expensive to obtain than long-term sources.

C Working-capital management is constrained by the liquidity and solvency subgoals of the firm, as well as the general economic conditions.

D Furthermore, specific uses and sources of funds are often cohesive and interdependent.

II Cash and marketable securities.

A The demand for liquid assets is normally attributed to three behavioral motives:

1 The transactions demand derives from the normal periodicity of payments on purchases.
2 The precautionary demand derives from the uncertainty of the origin and timing of cash flows.
3 The speculative demand derives from the desire to take advantage of expected changes in the price of assets.

B Since we are dealing primarily with nonfinancial corporations, primary emphasis will be placed on the transactions and precautionary demands.

1 Transactions needs are usually met with cash, i.e., currency and demand deposits.
2 Precautionary balances may be kept in highly marketable securities.

C The short-term management of funds involves the attainment of an optimal distribution between cash and marketable securities.

1 The risk of becoming technically insolvent must be considered against the expected return from investments of liquid funds in noncash uses.
2 However, most cash flows are typically determined by other functions within the firm, over which the financial manager has little control, or by outsiders, over which the manager has no control.
3 Furthermore, the financial manager must cope with seasonal and cyclical fluctuations as well as the fluctuations associated with the industry and overall economy.

D The maintenance of cash balances entails at least three types of costs:

1 The opportunity cost of foregoing lucrative investments.
2 The cost involved in holding cash that could be used to offset both the charges and financial risk that derives from the firm's short-term debt.
3 The costs involved with isolation from the short-term financial market due to the firm's excessive reliance on internally generated liquidity.

E Assuming that the cash flows and the relevant opportunity costs and benefits have been estimated, the financial manager should construct a model to determine the optimal cash-securities portfolio.

1 The critical minimum cash balance should be determined; it is the cash-floor constraint below which the firm incurs definite and measurable costs.
   (a) The critical minimum balance is justified by such institutional requirements as credit ratings, checking accounts, lines of credit, and risk aversion.
   (b) The short costs of a balance below the cash-floor constraint are determined by the actions of creditors and by the foregone cash discounts on the timely payment of accounts payable.
2 The short costs will be weighed against the opportunity costs of foregone investments.
3 The probabilistic model.
   (a) This model further assumes that all cash outflows can be deferred until the end of the planning period, that only one securities transaction is made, and that the securities are liquidated only at the end of the planning period.
   (b) The expected net cost, $E(C_n)$, of each alternative cash balance level can be computed with the following equation:

$$E(C_n) = E(S) + T - R$$

where $E(S)$ = expected total shortage cost of an alternative
T = transaction cost
R = known and certain return from investment of residual, short-term funds in securities

   (c) Choose the cash-securities portfolio that minimizes the expected net cost.
4 The Baumol method.
   (a) This method assumes that the cash is drawn evenly in lots of C dollars from other sources and uses; each borrowing has a fixed cost of b dollars; the cash payout over the planning period is a steady stream totaling T dollars; a composite interest rate, i, can be used instead of opportunity costs on individual investments.
   (b) The total transaction cost, TC, is computed with the formula below:

$$\text{TC} = bT/C + iC/2$$

where bT/C = total fixed cost for period
$iC/2$ = opportunity cost of maintaining average cash balance of $C/2$

   (c) The optimal borrowing lot size, $C*$, is found by differentiating the above equation with respect to C; that is,

$$C* = \sqrt{2bT/i}$$

   (d) The Baumol method, however, is severely limited by the following critical assumptions:
      (i) Disbursements are continuous over time.
      (ii) There are no unanticipated receipts.
      (iii) The costs of cash funds are constant.
      (iv) The transactions demand is the only motive for corporate cash holdings.

F There are certain steps the cash manager can follow to reduce the impact and cost of uncertainty.

1 By attempting to obtain an approximate coincidence of inflows and outflows of cash, he may reduce shortage costs.
2 He may attempt to reduce idle cash balances by shortening the time and distance traveled by the cash in the firm's daily operations.
3 The financial manager can attempt to reduce uncertainty by narrowing the variability of cash flows.

III Accounts receivable.

A The management of accounts receivable (credit-selling policy) involves a trade off between the benefits of the incremental profits from increased sales and the costs of the incremental expenditures on collection, bad debts, and opportunity costs.

B The appeal of investment in accounts receivable rests with the tendency of such policy to increase unit sales, even though it reduces the net unit profit.

1 There is a twofold effect in receivables investment:
(a) There is an increased sales effect that, given the same turnover in accounts receivable, will necessarily bring additional receivables.
(b) There is a slower average collection period that also increases the funds required to maintain the current receivables policy.
2 It is important to remember that the investment by the firm from an extension of credit does not require the entire new balance in average accounts receivable but, rather, only that portion which represents the cost of goods on account.

C The granting of discounts is also important in the control of funds through accounts receivable.

1 Discounts may have a considerable effect on product demand and the level of losses through bad debts.
2 Concern rests primarily on whether discounts will speed collection at a high enough rate to offset the costs of this policy.

D Another serious consideration in managing accounts receivable involves the assignment of correct probability estimates for expected bad-debt losses.

E It should be noted that an intensive collection policy may adversely affect sales.

IV Inventories.

A The need for inventories arises because the movement of economic goods through complex manufacturing and distribution processes requires time.

B The necessity of maintaining stocks of raw materials and finished goods gives rise to carrying costs and opportunity costs that vary directly with inventory size.

C The purchase of inventories involves a procurement cost that, on a per dollar basis, varies inversely with inventory size.

D The various uncertainties in the economy also give rise to stock costs.

1 It is often necessary to maintain buffer stocks to avoid shortage or stockout costs.
2 However, care must be taken to avoid equally damaging long or surplus costs.

E The EOQ model.

1 This model assumes a steady demand; no inventory reserves; a constant procurement cost, O; a constant carrying cost, C.
2 The total inventory cost, TIC, can be computed with the following equation:

$$\text{TCI} = CQ/2 + SO/Q$$

where Q = quantity of units ordered
S = total number of units required during planning period
$Q/2$ = average stock of goods
$CQ/2$ = approximate carrying cost
S/Q = total number of inventory orders
SO/Q = ordering cost

3 The optimal or economic order quantity (EOQ) is found by differentiating the above equation with respect to Q, setting the derivative equal to zero, and then solving for Q; that is,

$$\text{EOQ} = \sqrt{2SO/C}$$

4 The obvious shortcoming of the EOQ model is that most of the uncertainty is assumed away.
   (a) The uncertainty of inventory usage requires the maintenance of a safety stock whose level is determined by the probability distribution of the demand for the goods.
   (b) If it can be assumed that the required lead time for ordering goods is known and that demand quantities and shortage costs are fully quantifiable, then the uncertainty can be handled by enumerating all the alternative levels of inventory.
      (i) Develop a cost and a profit matrix for the various inventory levels.
      (ii) One may make the model more realistic by using a probabilistic delivery schedule to develop a schedule of estimated total inventory costs for each alternative.

QUESTIONS FOR SELF-EXAMINATION

True or False

_____ 1 Working-capital management is constrained by the liquidity and solvency subgoals of the firm.

_____ 2 The precautionary demand derives from the uncertainty of the origin and timing of cash flows.

_____ 3 Transactions needs are usually met with marketable securities.

_____ 4 The short costs of a balance below the cash-floor constraint are determined by the actions of creditors and by the foregone cash discounts.

_____ 5 The probabilistic model advocates the choice of the cash-securities portfolio that minimizes the expected net cost.

_____ 6 The total transaction cost computed by the Baumol method is composed of the total fixed cost for the planning period and the expected total shortage costs of the alternative cash balances.

_____ 7 The appeal of investment in accounts receivable rests with the tendency of such policy to increase the net unit profit.

_____ 8 The concern when granting discounts is whether they will speed collection at a high enough rate to offset the costs of this policy.

_____ 9 The various uncertainties in the economy give rise to inventory stockout and surplus costs.

_____ 10 The EOQ model and the Baumol method are essentially the products of the same technique applied to two different short-term uses of funds.

Multiple Choice

____ 1 The probabilistic model is dependent upon ______
(a) the probability distribution of the expected cash outflows.
(b) the magnitude of the shortage costs.
(c) the known and certain return from the investments in short-term securities.
(d) all the above.

____ 2 The need of the firm for liquid funds to pay for inputs to the production process is called the ______
(a) precautionary demand.
(b) transactions demand.
(c) solvency demand.
(d) speculative demand.

____ 3 The maintenance of cash balances entails all the costs listed below except the ______
(a) opportunity cost of foregoing lucrative investments.
(b) cost foregone by not using cash to offset the short-term debt charges of the firm.
(c) cost of foregone purchase discounts.
(d) cost involved with isolation from short-term financial markets.

____ 4 The Baumol method generalizes the concept of opportunity costs through the ______
(a) assumption that each borrowing has a fixed cost of b dollars.
(b) assumption that disbursements are continuous over time.
(c) assignment of a composite interest rate, i.
(d) assignment of evenly drawn lots of C dollars.

____ 5 The EOQ model enlarges the concept of inventory stock costs by assuming ______
(a) a steady demand.
(b) a constant carrying cost, C.
(c) a constant procurement cost, O.
(d) away uncertainty.

PROBLEMS FOR PRACTICE

1 The Flame Corporation is analyzing its cash balances. It currently holds a sizeable portfolio of marketable securities and withdraws funds from the portfolio as its cash needs dictate. Flame estimates its additional cash needs over the next year at $500,000. Its opportunity cost of holding cash is 4%. When marketable securities are liquidated, the company incurs a $25 fixed cost. Their minimum cash balance is set by company policy at $5,000. (a) Determine the optimal withdrawal size. (b) What will be the company's average cash balance? (c) How often during the year will Flame have to withdraw funds from its portfolio?

Solution

(a) $$C^* = \sqrt{\frac{2bT}{i}}$$

$$C^* = \sqrt{\frac{2 \times 25 \times 500{,}000}{.04}} = \sqrt{625{,}000{,}000} = \$25{,}000$$

(b) $$\text{Average cash balance} = \frac{\$25{,}000}{2} + \$5{,}000 = 12{,}500 + 5{,}000 = \$17{,}500$$

(c) $$\frac{\$500{,}000}{\$\ 25{,}000} = 20 \text{ times}$$

2 In a constantly changing world, Flame Corporation notes that the parameters in its cash-budgeting model are subject to change. Given the data in Problem 1, what is the effect on its

optimal withdrawal size, its average cash balance, and its number of withdrawals for the following changes: (a) Because of an increase in broker's commissions, the fixed cost of liquidating securities increases by $5. (b) Tight money conditions cause the opportunity cost of holding cash to increase to 5%. (c) Increased economic uncertainty prompts Flame to raise their minimum cash balance to $7,000.

Solution

(a) $C^* = \sqrt{\dfrac{2 \times (25 + 5) \times 500{,}000}{.04}} = \sqrt{750{,}000{,}000} = \$27{,}388$

Average cash balance $= \dfrac{\$27{,}388}{2} + \$5{,}000 = \$18{,}694$

$\dfrac{\$500{,}000}{\$\ 27{,}388} = 18.26$ times

(b) $C^* = \sqrt{\dfrac{2 \times 25 \times 500{,}000}{.05}} = \sqrt{500{,}000{,}000} = \$22{,}361$

Average cash balance $= \dfrac{\$22{,}361}{2} + \$5{,}000 = \$16{,}181$

$\dfrac{\$500{,}000}{\$\ 22{,}361} = 22.36$ times

(c) $C^* = \$25{,}000$ (no change)

Average cash balance $= \dfrac{\$25{,}000}{2} + \$7{,}000 = \$19{,}500$

$\dfrac{\$500{,}000}{\$\ 25{,}000} = 20$ times (no change)

3 Sight Company is considering a lock-box arrangement to improve the efficiency of converting their accounts receivable into cash. The First City Bank has agreed to such an arrangement providing Sight Company maintains a minimum balance of $90,000 in a deposit account. The financial manager of Sight estimates their float could be reduced from seven to four days. If they have average daily receipts of $50,000 and the released funds are used to repay a 7% bank loan, what are the savings from the lock-box arrangement?

Solution

$50,000 × 3 days = $150,000 cash released

$150,000 − $90,000 = $60,000 net cash released

$60,000 × .07 = $4,200 savings realized

4 Cash Sales, Inc. is giving serious thought to changing their cash-only credit policy to one with terms of net 30. They estimate that their annual sales will increase from $2.5 million to $3 million based on a sales price of $25 per unit and that all customers will take advantage of the 30-day credit period. At their current level of sales, fixed costs and variable costs are $7 and $16 per unit, respectively. If this new credit policy is adopted, what is the rate of return on investment in accounts receivable for cash sales?

Solution

Current sales	$2,500,000/$25 = 100,000 units	
New sales	$3,000,000/$25 = 120,000 units	
Total fixed costs	100,000 units × $ 7 =	$ 700,000
Total variable costs	120,000 units × $16 =	1,920,000
Total costs (at new sales level)		$2,620,000

Total average cost = $2,620,000/120,000 units = $21.83/unit

$$\text{Average accounts receivable} = \frac{\$3{,}00\text{C}{,}000}{360/30} = \$250{,}000$$

$$\text{Additional investment in accounts receivable} = \frac{\$21.83}{\$25} \times \$250{,}000 = \$218{,}300$$

$$\text{Incremental profit} = 20{,}000 \text{ units} \times (\$25 - \$16) = \$180{,}000$$

$$\text{Rate of return} = \frac{\text{incremental profits}}{\text{additional investment}} = \frac{\$180{,}000}{\$218{,}000} = .825 = 82.5\%$$

5 Gomey Sporting Goods manufactures 1,000 wooden tennis rackets every three months. These rackets necessitate total purchases of 450 pounds of high quality wood. Each shipment of wood incurs ordering costs of $20, and the inventory carrying costs per pound of wood are $2 per month. What is the economic order quantity of the wood and the total inventory costs during the three months?

Solution

$$\text{EOQ} = \sqrt{2SO/C} = \sqrt{\frac{2 \times 450 \times \$20}{\$2 \times 3 \text{ months}}} = \sqrt{3{,}000} = 54.78 \text{ pounds}$$

$$\text{TIC} = \frac{CQ}{2} + \frac{SO}{Q} = \frac{\$6 \times 54.78}{2} + \frac{450 \times \$20}{54.78} = \$164.34 + \$164.29 = \$328.63$$

6 The Flue Chemical Company anticipates the following demand schedule for its sodium chloride:

Quantity demanded (barrels)	100	110	120	130
Probability	.2	.4	.3	.1

Its associated shortage and carrying costs are $5 per barrel and $3 per barrel, respectively. The gross profit per barrel is $22. Determine the optimum level of sodium chloride inventory.

Solution

Cost matrix for various levels of inventory:

Let X = inventory strategy, Y = demand

When $X = Y$, cost = $0
$X > Y$, cost = $(X - Y)$ ($3)
$X < Y$, cost = $(Y - X)$ ($5)

Cost matrix:

X \ Y	*100*	*110*	*120*	*130*
100	0	50	100	150
110	30	0	50	100
120	60	30	0	50
130	90	60	30	0

Payoff matrix for various levels of inventory:

When $X = Y$, payoff = X($12)
$X > Y$, payoff = Y($12) — cost matrix element
$X < Y$, payoff = X($12) — cost matrix element

Payoff matrix:

Y / X	100	110	120	130	
		Probabilities			*Expected*
	.2	*.4*	*.3*	*.1*	*Value*
100	1,200	1,150	1,100	1,050	$1,135
110	1,170	1,320	1,270	1,220	1,265
120	1,140	1,290	1,440	1,390	1,315*
130	1,110	1,260	1,410	1,560	1,305

The optimum level of inventory is 120 barrels of sodium chloride since it yields the highest expected payoff, denoted by the value with an asterisk.

PROBLEMS FOR SELF-EXAMINATION

7 Firm A estimates its additional cash needs over the next period at $125,000. It decides to borrow the necessary funds from the bank at 9% and to invest the funds in Treasury Bills yielding 4%. The bank charges a fixed processing fee of $18 each time funds are withdrawn. Calculate the optimum borrowing amount for Firm A.

Solution

$$C^* = \sqrt{\frac{2bT}{i}}$$

$$= \sqrt{\frac{2 \times \$\qquad\qquad \times \$\qquad\qquad}{(.09 - \qquad\qquad)}}$$

$$= \sqrt{\qquad\qquad\qquad}$$

= $ optimum borrowing size

8 The Seer Company has $21.6 million in credit sales with an average float of three days. They have a lock-box arrangement with First City Bank with the requirement that they maintain a $40,000 minimum balance in a deposit account. Their opportunity cost of holding cash balances is 5%, and they realized a $4,000 savings after instituting the lock-box arrangement. Based on this information, how many days of float was Seer Company experiencing prior to the lock-box arrangement?

Solution

9 The Ace Machine Company has been selling its machines on the terms of net 20. An analysis of their current situation indicates that changing their credit terms to 2/10, net 30 will increase sales from 600 to 800 units per year. However, it will also increase the firm's average collection period from 20 to 30 days and their bad debt losses from 2% to 5%. It is anticipated that 40% of their customers (in dollar volume) will take advantage of the discount. The sales price of each machine is $1,200 with $200 per unit and $800 per unit representing the fixed and variable costs, respectively. What are the gross benefits and costs of adopting the new credit policy?

Solution

10 The Northern Snowmobile Company is attempting to estimate the number of snowmobiles to stock for the month of November. The demand for snowmobiles is dependent upon whether the area receives a heavy early snow. Bearing this in mind, their estimated demand schedule is as follows:

Quantity	20	30	40	50
Probability	.3	.4	.2	.1

The gross profit per snowmobile is $50, and the shortage and carrying costs are $15 and $20 per unit, respectively. What level of inventory do you recommend?

Solution

Cost matrix:

Payoff matrix:

12 Short-Term Sources of Funds

Theme Chapter 12 discusses the other half of working-capital management, that is, short-term sources of funds. Specifically, five important short-term sources are presented: trade credit, unsecured bank loans, commercial paper, accounts receivable financing, and inventory financing.

I Trade credit refers to the sale of goods on noncash terms.

A This short-term source of financing is the most common, easy to obtain, and sizable in dollar volume.

B The three basic categories of trade credit are open accounts, notes payable, and trade acceptances.

1 Open accounts, better known as accounts payable, are almost automatically dictated by the terms of sale; there is no formal agreement.
2 Notes payable, or promissory notes, are used when formal acknowledgment of debt is desirable; the formality provides the lender with increased enforcement power.
3 Trade acceptances are formal agreements in which the delivery of goods is not completed until the buyer accepts a draft drawn by the seller; the draft requires the buyer to designate a bank where the debt repayment will be arranged.

C Open-end trade credit — the most popular form of trade credit — is determined by four factors:

1 The nature of the product — products with a high turnover are sold on shorter credit terms than those with low turnover.
2 The seller's financial position — a seller with a strong current asset position can extend more favorable credit terms than a seller with a weak position.
3 The buyer's financial condition — a buyer with a strong market position is likely to exercise greater scrutiny in searching for credit than a weak buyer whose alternatives are limited.
4 The terms of sale — by controlling the attractiveness of the cash discount, the seller can often influence the buyer's choice of credit terms.

D The advantages of open accounts include ready availability and flexibility. The costs of open accounts are described below.

1 When a discount is offered but not utilized, the cost of credit is the annualized discount cost, which may be viewed as a penalty.
2 Credit costs depend upon the relation between the date when a good is purchased and the billing dates of the seller.

E Some complications associated with the use of open accounts are

1 If the cost of credit is included in the price of a good, analysis of credit costs is more difficult. The buyer must compare the prices and credit terms of many sellers to discern the best purchase.
2 Another credit cost that is difficult to analyze is the opportunity cost involved in stretching payments past the "net" period.

F The trade-credit policy of the firm has important implications for the management of short-term funds.

1 Taking advantage of cash discounts involves an added cash outflow.
2 The availability and size of trade credit will affect the average level of cash balances.
3 The availability and size of trade credit will affect the firm's own trade-credit policy to others.
4 The terms that the firm can secure through its trade-credit policy will influence the carrying costs of its inventories and may well affect the size of its inventories.

G In the final analysis, the question of trade-credit costs is rather trivial because they are often unavoidable.

1 Of greater importance is the management of the marginal portion of credit.
2 This analysis involves the decision to take advantage of a discount or to incur the penalty.

II Typically, there are three types of (short-term) unsecured bank loans: a line of credit, a revolving credit agreement, and a transaction loan.

A A line of credit is an informal agreement with a ceiling on the credit availability.

1 Many banks require the borrowing firm to be free of the bank debt sometime during the fiscal period.
2 There is no legal obligation on the part of the bank to extend the promised credit.

B The revolving credit agreement usually requires a fee on the unused portion of the total credit, involves a legal commitment for the bank, and may extend beyond a year.

C The transaction loan is undertaken when a firm needs funds for a specific purpose; its primary determinant is the bank's evaluation of the future cash flows of the specific project.

D The cost of bank loans is determined largely by the market interest rate.

1 The interest rate charged usually depends upon the credit worthiness of the firm and the prime interest rate.
2 Commercial banks typically require the borrowing firm to maintain a compensating balance, i.e., a minimum demand deposit balance that is normally a percentage of the total loan commitment. This arrangement raises the effective cost of bank loans.
3 The true loan cost also depends upon the methods of assessing charges and repayment.
   (a) If a loan is discounted, the interest charge is deducted in advance and, hence, increases the effective cost of the loan.
   (b) If a loan is repayable on an installment basis, the effective annual cost is approximately doubled because the average balance outstanding is halved.

E There are certain benefits in dealing with a bank.

1 A good relationship with a sizable bank may be translated into credit availability during periods of tight money.
2 A steady relationship is likely to produce technical advice, business contacts, and so on.

III Commercial paper consists of the unsecured promissory notes of large firms that are sold primarily to other large firms and financial institutions.

A Since the notes are not secured and are sold in a third market, only the most credit-worthy firms are able to use this source of funds.

B Commercial paper is available through dealers who function primarily as brokers and through direct placement to the lender.

1 The market for commercial paper is highly organized and sophisticated; most paper is sold in $25,000 denominations.
2 Alternatively, the direct-placement market is composed of large sales-finance companies that tailor the maturity and amount of the notes to the needs of investors.

C Commercial paper is usually 1% to 2% cheaper than unsecured bank loans and is a larger source of funds.

D However, the impersonal nature of this market provides for little or no negotiation, and excessive reliance on it may isolate the firm from its sources in the banking industry.

IV Accounts receivable financing is the pledge of accounts receivable as a means of securing a loan; the lender will consider the average quality and size of these accounts in determining the percentage of their face value that he will lend.

A Accounts receivable financing can be facilitated by an assignment of an account or by the factoring of receivables.

1 The assignment of an account requires the borrower to sign a promissory note and a security agreement; the assignment may be arranged on either a notification or non-notification basis.
(a) Under the notification method, the buyer of the merchandise is notified of the assignment of his account and makes his payments directly to the lender.
(b) Under the nonnotification method, the buyer of the merchandise is not notified of the assignment and continues to make payments to the borrower, who forwards them to the lender.
2 The factoring of receivables involves the transfer of the title of the receivables to a factor who manages and collects the account.
(a) The lending institution bears the collection costs and the bad-debt losses.
(b) However, the factor may be employed for a flat fee of about 2% of the receivables to perform only the collection and risk-bearing functions, without the lending responsibilities.

B There are several advantages to short-term financing through receivables:

1 It gives the borrowing firm flexibility since financing can vary with sales.
2 It relieves the borrowing firm of substantial collection and credit-risk costs.
3 It is often ideally suited and perhaps the only alternative for small and financially weak firms.

C There are two disadvantages:

1 Since the cost of borrowing alone is several points higher than the prime rate, accounts receivable financing is very costly.
2 By financing its own receivables, the firm weakens its credit worthiness to banks and other institutional creditors.

V Inventory financing, of which there are four kinds, varies with the credit worthiness of the firm, the type of inventory secured, and the custodian involved.

A A floating lien may be attached on all the inventories of the firm.

1 Furthermore, this arrangement may be extended to cover any length of time as well as accounts receivable.
2 However, because it is costly or impossible to exercise control over the collateral, this arrangement is vague and provides little security for the lender.

B A trust receipt transfers title of the merchandise to the lender and allows the borrower to hold them in trust.

1 This arrangement provides more control for the lender in that he has a definite means of access to the specific collateral.
2 However, effective control over the care and disposition of the collateral is still difficult.

C Terminal warehousing requires the borrower to store his inventory in a public warehouse, which issues a receipt to the lender known as a terminal warehouse receipt.

1 The warehouse will release the inventory to the borrower only on the explicit authorization of the lender.
2 Although this arrangement gives the lender strict control over the collateral, it is inflexible and excessively costly to the borrower.

D Field warehousing allows for loans to be made against inventories that remain on the premises of the borrower.

1 The lender contracts the services of a third party, i.e., the field warehousing company, to act as a control agent.
2 This arrangement is also distinguished by public notification of the arrangement.
3 Since financing is tied to the growth of the inventories and related directly to the needs of the borrower, field warehousing provides considerable flexibility.
4 Although improved warehousing practices reduce both losses and labor costs, it is still a high-cost source of short-term funds.

QUESTIONS FOR SELF-EXAMINATION

True or False

_____ 1 Open accounts are readily available, flexible, and almost automatically dictated by the terms of sale.

_____ 2 When a discount is offered but not utilized, the cost of credit is the foregone saving on the price of the merchandise.

_____ 3 A line of credit contains no legal obligation for the bank to extend the promised credit.

_____ 4 Because a revolving credit agreement may extend beyond a year, it can cease to be a short-term source of funds.

_____ 5 If a loan is repayable on an installment basis, the effective annual cost is approximately halved because the average balance outstanding is doubled.

_____ 6 Only the most credit-worthy firms are able to use commercial paper as a short-term source of funds.

_____ 7 Accounts receivable and inventory financing involve the pledge of the account as a means of securing a loan.

_____ 8 A trust receipt is the formal acknowledgment of a terminal warehousing arrangement.

_____ 9 Although terminal warehousing requires the borrower to store his inventory in a public warehouse, he may acquire it whenever he wishes.

_____ 10 The interest rate charged on unsecured bank loans primarily depends upon the credit worthiness of the firm and the prime interest rate.

Multiple Choice

_____ 1 _____ is the most common, easy to obtain, and sizable in dollar volume of the short-term sources of funds.

(a) Accounts receivable financing
(b) Commercial paper
(c) Trade credit
(d) Inventory financing

_____ 2 Which of the following factors is not a determinant of open-end trade credit?

(a) The prime interest rate
(b) The terms of sale
(c) The nature of the merchandise
(d) The seller's financial position

_____ 3 The _____ is undertaken when a firm needs funds for a specific purpose.

(a) assignment of an account
(b) transaction loan
(c) floating lien
(d) promissory note

_____ 4 Which of the following is not an advantage to short-term financing through receivables?

(a) It permits the firm to finance its own receivables.
(b) It allows financing to vary with sales.
(c) It relieves the borrowing firm of collection and credit-risk costs.
(d) It is particularly suited to small and financially weak firms.

_____ 5 The _____ is tied to the growth of inventories and is directly related to the needs of the borrower.

(a) trust receipt arrangement
(b) commercial paper arrangement
(c) trade acceptance agreement
(d) field warehousing arrangement

PROBLEMS FOR PRACTICE

1 Determine the effective annual interest rate of not taking the cash discount given the following credit terms:

(a) 2/10, net 30
(b) 2/10, net 60
(c) 1/10, net 60
(d) 4/10, net 30
(e) net 60
(f) 5/10, net 60

Solution

(a) $\frac{2}{100-2} \times \frac{360}{30-10} = \frac{2}{98} \times \frac{360}{20} = 36.73\%$

(b) $\frac{2}{100-2} \times \frac{360}{60-10} = \frac{2}{98} \times \frac{360}{50} = 14.69\%$

(c) $\frac{1}{100-1} \times \frac{360}{60-10} = \frac{1}{99} \times \frac{360}{50} = 7.27\%$

(d) $\frac{4}{100-4} \times \frac{360}{30-15} = \frac{4}{96} \times \frac{360}{15} = 100.00\%$

(e) 0%, no cash discount is offered

(f) $\frac{5}{100-5} \times \frac{360}{60-10} = \frac{5}{95} \times \frac{360}{50} = 37.89\%$

2 Firm A borrows $100,000 from First City Bank for one year at 8% interest. The bank requires the company to maintain a 20% compensating balance in a demand deposit account. (a) What is the amount Firm A has available for use, and what is the effective annual interest rate? (b) If Firm A requires the $100,000 to pay another creditor, what is the total amount it has to borrow? What is the effective annual interest rate?

Solution

(a) $100,000 − (.20 × $100,000) = $80,000 available for use

$$\frac{.08 \times \$100{,}000}{\$80{,}000} = 10\% \text{ effective interest rate}$$

(b) X = total amount borrowed

$X - .20X = \$100{,}000 \qquad .80X = \$100{,}000$

$X = \$100{,}000/.80 = \$125{,}000$ total amount borrowed

$$\frac{.08 \times \$125{,}000}{\$100{,}000} = 10\% \text{ effective interest rate}$$

3 The Block Company is borrowing $70,000 from their local banker. The bank charges 7.5% interest and discounts the loan. (a) Determine the funds available for use and the effective rate of interest. (b) If, in addition, the bank requires a 10% compensating balance, calculate the effective rate of interest.

Solution

(a) $70,000 − (.075 × $70,000) = $70,000 − $5,250
= $64,750 available for use

$$\frac{\$5{,}250}{\$64{,}750} = 8.11\% \text{ effective interest rate}$$

(b) $$\frac{\$5{,}250}{\$64{,}750 - (.10 \times \$70{,}000)} = \frac{5{,}250}{57{,}750} = 9.09\% \text{ effective interest rate}$$

4 The Green Fabric Company factors their accounts receivable. Their average accounts receivable are $120,000 with terms of net 30. The factor charges a $100 per month service fee and 1% per month interest rate. Calculate the effective annual rate of interest for factoring. The service fee is not discounted from the amount loaned to Green Fabric.

Solution

Monthly interest = $120,000 × .01 =	$1,200
Service fee	100
Total monthly cost	$1,300

$$\frac{\$1{,}300}{\$120{,}000} \times 12 \text{ months} = 1.083\% \times 12 = 12.996\% \text{ effective annual rate of interest}$$

5 Hess Variety, Inc. is considering two ways of acquiring needed funds. They can borrow $200,000 from their bank at 8% interest with a 15% compensating balance. A local finance company will lend them 80% of the face value of their average accounts receivable. The finance company charges a $200 service fee per month discounted from the loan and .75% per month interest. Their average accounts receivable are $300,000. Which financing alternative has the lower effective rate of interest?

Solution

Bank loan:

$200,000 × .08 = $16,000 interest costs
$200,000 − (.15 × $200,000) = $200,000 − $30,000
= $170,000 available for use

$$\frac{\$16{,}000}{\$170{,}000} = 9.41\% \text{ effective annual rate of interest.}$$

Accounts receivable financing:

Amount available for loan = $300,000 × .80 = $240,000
Amount loaned = $240,000 − $200 = $239,800

Monthly interest = $239,800 × .0075 =	$1,799
Service fee	200
Total monthly costs	$1,999

$$\frac{\$1{,}999}{\$239{,}800} = .834 \times 12 \text{ months}$$

$$= 10.01\% \text{ effective annual rate of interest}$$

Since the bank loan has the lowest effective rate of interest, it should be selected as the proper financing alternative.

PROBLEMS FOR SELF-EXAMINATION

6 A company has purchased supplies worth $10,000 from Firm A on terms of 3/10, net 45 and materials worth $10,000 from Firm B on terms of 2/20, net 45. The company, however, has sufficient cash to pay only one creditor within the discount period. (a) Which firm should the company pay? (b) If the company can borrow funds from their bank at 12% to take advantage of the discount offered, what is the amount of savings realized?

Solution

(a)

(b)

7 The Gore Company has negotiated a $125,000 loan with their banker. The terms are 8% interest with a 15% compensating balance. Gore Company currently maintains a $10,000 minimum cash balance on account with the bank. Determine the effective rate of interest of the loan.

Solution

8 Candlestick Company has annual credit sales of $300,000 and an average collection period of 30 days. They factor their receivables with the First Finance Company on a continuing basis. First charges a $100 per month collection fee and 1% per month interest rate on the loaned funds. Determine the effective annual rate of interest Candlestick pays for factoring their receivables.

Solution

13 Valuation of the Firm: The Case for Fundamental Analysis

Theme An appreciation of the valuation methods employed by investors is necessary before the firm can establish an efficient set of financial goals. In line with this, Chapter 13 introduces the three major approaches to security valuation: technical, fundamental, and random walk. The fundamental method will be discussed here; the other two methods are reviewed in the next chapter.

I The theory of share-price valuation is founded on the proposition that certain relevant variables and relationships exist and can be used in a valuation model, of which there are two general types.

A Quantitative models are developed on the premise that the actions of investors can be explained in terms of certain quantifiable variables and their relationships.

1 They are totally dependent upon the current value of the relevant variables.
2 Future share prices are determined by estimating the expected value of the variables, substituting these values into the specific model, and solving for share price in terms of these estimates.

B Qualitative models are based on historical patterns of price-volume relationships and market psychology.

1 Some of these models incorporate the past price-volume relationships in an attempt to predict the behavioral patterns of investors.
2 Other qualitative models are based on the belief that stock market psychology and the resultant share-price movements are determined primarily by national and international political and economic states described in daily news releases.

II The discipline of security valuation is usually classified into three different approaches: the technical, fundamental, and random-walk approaches.

A Because it is interested in the behavioral reactions of investors to historical trends and patterns, the technical approach is a qualitative model-building method.

B Because they do not rely on past market behavior to determine future share prices, the fundamental and random-walk approaches are quantitative model-building methods.

C One of the earliest fundamental models was developed by Tinbergen.

1 He postulated that stock prices vary directly with dividends and inversely with long-term interest rates.
2 The Tinbergen dynamic model is

$$P_o = f(x,y,z)$$

where P_o = share price
x = long-term interest rates
y = dividend yields on nominal investment
z = rate of change in share price

D Another early fundamental model was proposed by Williams.

1 He suggested that the value of a security may be determined by the perpetual summation of the discounted, anticipated dividends.
2 His model is

$$P = \sum_{t=1}^{\infty} \overline{R}_t/(1 + k)^t$$

where P = share price
$\overline{R}_t$ = expected value of return in year t
k = discount rate

E Like the other two approaches, the random-walk approach has many variations.

1 A narrow interpretation of the random-walk hypothesis suggests that future price changes are independent of past price movements; hence, historical data are not useful in predicting future states.
2 A broader interpretation suggests that present prices fully reflect all public information; hence, equity markets allocate resources efficiently.

III The proponents of the fundamental approach to security valuation believe that stock prices are reflections of the intrinsic value of the corporation.

A The basic problem is to determine what investors really capitalize when they make their decisions in the market.

B Practitioners of fundamental valuation believe that stock price levels and movements can be explained and predicted in terms of the expectations of the investing public concerning future dividends, earnings, growth rates, and investment opportunities.

IV Dividend valuation models are built on the assumption that investors purchase a security for the expected flow of dividends.

A Therefore, share prices are determined by capitalizing the future dividend stream at a particular capitalization rate.

B This rate is typically dependent upon the industry in which the firm operates and the estimated uncertaintv of the dividend stream.

C Two examples of dividend valuation models are

1 The Gordon and Shapiro model, assuming a firm without debt, proposes the present market value of a security to be the discounted stream of expected dividends.
(a) Specifically, the equation for the model is

$$P_o = D_o/(k - g)$$

where P_o = present market value of a security
D_o = dividend per share
k = market rate of discount
g = growth rate of dividends

(b) If one also assumes that the firm anticipates a constant rate of return, r, and a constant retention rate, b, then all future dividends will result from the reinvestment of retained earnings; that is,

$$P_o = (1 - b)rA_o/(k - rb)$$

where A_o = total assets of firm
g = product of rate of return and retention rate, rb

2 The Walter model assumes that corporate dividend policies are guided by the goal of maximizing the wealth of the common stockholders.

(a) Specifically, the equation for the model is

$$P_c = E/B_c + [(B_a - B_c)/B_c^2](E - D) \quad \text{or}$$

$$P_c = E/B_c + (E - D)(B_a - B_c)/B_c^2$$

where P_c = market value of company's common stock
E = earnings per share
B_c = market discount rate
B_a = productivity of retained earnings or growth rate
D = dividend per share

(b) In the above equation, the first term is the summation of the discounted future earnings, and the second term is the present value of the cash flow generated by the earnings retained for reinvestment.

(c) In effect, then, the discounted sum of both terms assigns a value to a share of common stock equal to the anticipated dividends and the growth of dividends.

V Earnings valuation models have been developed on the proposition that the market value of a security is determined by the present value of all properly adjusted, anticipated earnings.

A The stream of earnings model can be expressed as

$$P_t = \sum_{t=1}^{\infty} (E_t - I_t)/(1 + k)^t$$

where P_t = market share price in period t
E_t = earnings per share at period t
I_t = investment per share at period t
k = market discount rate

B In other words, the market value of a company's shares is determined by the present value of the expected stream of earnings minus the investment costs, with both factors properly adjusted.

VI The discounted-cash-flow approach to security valuation equates a firm's equity with the present value of all future cash flows to the stockholders.

A Bodenhorn's model is an example of this approach and is developed along three related concepts:

1 The *stockholders' initial investment* is expressed as

$$P_o = \sum_{i=1}^{\infty} CF_i/(1 + k)^i$$

where P_o = initial investment of a shareholder
CF_i = net cash flows anticipated in future periods
k = market discount rate

2 Since an investor expects a return during his holding period, the *stockholders' expected end-of-period wealth* is expressed as

$$E(W_1) = \sum_{i=1}^{\infty} \overline{CF}_i/(1 + \overline{k})^{i-1}$$

where $E(W_1)$ = expected wealth at end of investment horizon
$\overline{CF}_i, \overline{k}$ = expected values of respective variables

3 The *stockholders' actual end-of-period wealth* is expressed as

$$W_1 = CF_1 + P_1$$

where W_1 = actual wealth
CF_1 = actual cash flow during period 1
P_1 = actual market share price at end of period 1

(a) Under conditions of certainty, expected and actual wealth will be equal.
(b) However, under conditions of uncertainty, expected and actual wealth may differ because $\overline{CF}_1 \neq CF_1$ or because $\bar{k} \neq k$.

B The discounted-cash-flow technique, though, does not really shed significant light on the investment criteria of investors.

VII The investment-opportunities model proposes the market value of a corporate share to be the sum of the present value of both the constant earnings from currently held assets and the earnings from all future investment projects undertaken.

VIII Cost-of-capital valuation models relate the cost of equity capital to certain variables that specify the firm's performance in terms of risk-return characteristics.

A The Miller and Modigliani model specifies the value of a firm as a function of current earnings and investment opportunities.

B Their model is expressed as

$$P(0) = \sum_{t=0}^{\infty} [E(t) - I(t)]/(1 + k)^{t+1}$$

where $P(0)$ = market value of firm at time 0
$E(t)$ = earnings in period t
$I(t)$ = investment in additional physical assets
k = investor's discount rate

C According to the Miller and Modigliani framework, a stockholder should be indifferent among the financing of new investments through retention, the issuance of new equity to the existing stockholders, or both the above.

IX The models of security valuation presented differ primarily only in the measures of return used; indeed, the measures of return — dividends, earnings, and capital gains — are equivalent.

QUESTIONS FOR SELF-EXAMINATION

True or False

_____ 1 Qualitative models are totally dependent upon the current value of the relevant variables.

_____ 2 One interpretation of the random-walk hypothesis suggests that future price changes are independent of past price movements.

_____ 3 The basic problem of security valuation is to determine what investors really capitalize when they make their decisions in the market.

_____ 4 Dividend valuation models determine share prices by capitalizing the future dividend stream of a security at a particular capitalization rate.

_____ 5 The discounted-cash-flow approach equates the benefits from all cash flows to the stockholder with their costs.

_____ 6 Cost-of-capital valuation models discount the total net worth of the firm with the equity capitalization rate.

_____ 7 Essentially, the security valuation models presented in this chapter are equivalent.

____ 8 In one of the earliest fundamental models, Tinbergen postulated stock prices to vary directly with long-term interest rates and inversely with dividends.

____ 9 In effect, the Walter model assigns a value to a share of common stock equal to the expected dividends and the growth of dividends.

____ 10 The discounted-cash-flow technique is more a description of investor behavior than an explanation or analysis of it.

Multiple Choice

____ 1 Fundamentalists believe that stock price levels and movements can be explained and predicted in terms of ________

(a) historical patterns of price-volume relationships.
(b) the expectations of investors.
(c) market psychology.
(d) both (a) and (c).

____ 2 The Gordon and Shapiro model proposes the present market value of a security to be the ________

(a) discounted stream of expected dividends.
(b) present value of all properly adjusted, anticipated earnings.
(c) stockholders' expected end-of-period wealth.
(d) sum of current earnings and the earnings from future investments.

____ 3 Cost-of-capital valuation models relate the cost of equity capital to certain variables that specify the firm's performance in terms of ____

(a) total earnings.
(b) the total dividend paid.
(c) its growth rate.
(d) risk-return characteristics.

____ 4 The Miller and Modigliani model is a cost-of-capital model but is very nearly the same as which other model of security valuation?

(a) The earnings valuation model
(b) The investment-opportunities model
(c) The dividend valuation model
(d) None of the above

PROBLEMS FOR PRACTICE

1 GT, Inc. is currently paying a $2.75 dividend per share and anticipates it to grow at 8% per year. The market is discounting similar firms at a 12% rate. According to the Gordon-Shapiro model, determine the market price per share of GT stock.

Solution

$$P_o = \frac{D_o}{k - g} = \frac{\$2.75}{.12 - .08} = \frac{2.75}{.04} = \$68.75$$

2 Sandra Shrewd analyzes potential investments with the Walter model. Her study of Dot Motors indicates that the past five years growth rate of 9% should continue. The earnings per share anticipated are $3.20, and the company's policy is to pay out 40% in dividends. Sandra requires a 12% return from such an investment. What is the maximum amount that Sandra will pay for Dot Motors?

Solution

$$D = \$3.20 \times .40 = \$1.28$$

$$P_c = \frac{E}{B_c} + \frac{B_a - B_c}{B_c^2}(E - D)$$

$$= \frac{\$3.20}{.12} + \frac{.09 - .12}{(.12)^2}(\$3.20 - \$1.28)$$

$$= 26.67 + (-4.00) = \$22.67$$

Sandra will not pay more than $22.67 for Dot Motors.

3 High-Rise, Inc. is a rapidly growing company. The last 12 months earnings per share were $4.50, and they are anticipated to grow at a 20% rate for the next five years. High-Rise has a payout ratio of 15%, retaining the balance to invest in the firm's growth. A security analyst has estimated the market price of High-Rise to be $120 per share in three years. Based on the earnings valuation model, what is an appropriate price today if the market discounts the stock at 18%?

Solution

$E_0 = \$4.50$ | $I_0 = 4.50(1 - .15) = \$3.83$

$E_1 = 4.50(1 + .2) = \$5.40$ | $I_1 = 5.40(1 - .15) = \$4.59$

$E_2 = 5.40(1 + .2) = \$6.48$ | $I_2 = 6.48(1 - .15) = \$5.51$

$E_3 = 6.48(1 + .2) = \$7.78$ | $I_3 = 7.78(1 - .15) = \$6.61$

$P_3 = \$120$ | $k = .18$

$$P_0 = \frac{E_1 - I_1}{(1+k)^1} + \frac{E_2 - I_2}{(1+k)^2} + \frac{E_3 - I_3}{(1+k)^3} + \frac{P_3}{(1+k)^3}$$

$$= \frac{5.40 - 4.59}{(1 + .18)^1} + \frac{6.48 - 5.51}{(1 + .18)^2} + \frac{7.78 - 6.61}{(1 + .18)^3} + \frac{120}{(1 + .18)^3}$$

$$= \frac{.81}{1.180} + \frac{.97}{1.392} + \frac{1.17}{1.643} + \frac{120}{1.643} = .69 + .70 + .71 + 73.04$$

$= \$75.14$ appropriate current market price

PROBLEMS FOR SELF-EXAMINATION

4 The earnings per share of Shawl Company have grown from $2.20 five years ago to its current $3.23. During this period the company maintained a 50% dividend payout. Assuming that the historical growth rate and dividend payout will continue and that the market discounts the stock at 14%, determine its current market value using the Gordon-Shapiro model.

Solution

98 5 An investor purchased shares of Box Company at $28 per share with the expectation of obtaining a 10% return. Based on their past growth rate of 6%, Box Company anticipates earning $3 per share and returning $1.20 in dividends to their stockholders. Using the Walter model for valuation, was the investor's purchase a wise one?

Solution

14 Valuation of the Firm: The Case for Technical and Random-Walk Approaches

Theme Since fundamental theorists have never seriously claimed enough precision in the specification of their models for market estimation, attention has turned to the other two approaches to security valuation: the technical and random-walk approaches.

I The followers of the technical methodology are typically called technicians because of their preoccupation with past price patterns and movements.

A The chartist, the best known representative of this approach, believes that future share prices can be predicted from their past price movements.

1 This belief is based on the proposition that certain identifiable, recurrent patterns of price movements exist and can be used to predict the future movements and trends of speculative prices.
2 The chartist typically maintains a graphic record of a security's daily or weekly price, trading range, and volume traded.
3 A chartist predicts without regard to news releases, earnings, dividends, or growth prospects.
4 His forecasting method is not definite or precise but, rather, a sort of "eyeballing" technique that is more of an art than a discipline.
(a) Predictions are based on a belief in recurrent trends and the continuity of trends once they emerge.
(b) In spite of its modest popularity, stock charting remains a very inexact technique and does not lend itself to making sound investment decisions.

B Basic to the technical approach is the belief that enough imperfection exists in capital markets to allow trends to persist long enough for the technician to reap the profits of his foresight and synchronization.

II The proponents of the random-walk approach refute the usefulness of either public or privileged information in forecasting market values.

A The theory of random walks is based on two hypotheses:

1 Successive price changes in the various stock exchanges are independent of previous movements.
2 Security price changes conform to some probability distribution.

B The economic interpretation of the random-walk theory is founded on the proposition that speculative markets allocate resources efficiently.

1 As a result of perfect availability, efficient dissemination, and correct evaluation of

information by the market participants, price changes in a given period reflect only new information.

2 The informed participants will eliminate all profits in excess of the bare minimum required to induce them to continue in the market.

III Some empirical evidence on the random-walk theory is mentioned below.

A The original analytical and empirical work was done by Bachelier in 1900; he suggested that the expected profits to a stock market speculator should be equal to zero.

B Working, in 1934, noticed that changes between successive items in time series tended to be largely random.

C Osborne later suggested that it was not absolute price changes which are independent but changes in the logarithm of prices; these changes are approximately equivalent to proportionate changes in stock prices.

D Arnold Moore, in 1962, verified Osborne's results but also uncovered some evidence that there existed a consistent tendency for more large price changes than expected under the assumption of a normal distribution.

IV Some empirical tests on the two hypotheses underlying the random-walk approach are

A In his test for the nonlinear dependence in stock prices, Sidney Alexander concluded that speculative asset price changes follow a random walk, but that once a change is initiated, it tends to persist.

B Cootner showed that simple market rules can, on an overall basis, do substantially better than the buy-and-hold policy, thus pointing to the existence of either dependence or nonstationarity.

C In another study by Osborne, the conclusion was that transactions were not independent of past history; i.e., trading tends to come in bursts.

V A functional synthesis of the important variables that enter the valuation process requires the construction of a stock valuation model which links the investment and financing decisions of the firm.

A Sloane and Reisman have attempted to reconcile and generalize the various hypotheses regarding the independent variables that enter into a stock valuation model.

1 The generalized framework developed by Sloane and Reisman is known by the acronym DECP LION.

(a) DECP implies a reconciliation of the dividend, earnings, and cash-flow hypotheses in a finite-horizon context.

(b) LION implies the ability to finance investment opportunities through debt, retention, and the sale of new equity.

2 In the case where the various methods of valuation, DECP, and financing, LION, are equally weighted, the generalization reduces to the net-cash-flow approach; by allowing for the assignment of unequal weights to the various methods of financing, the framework implicitly accounts for both the availability and cost of each source of funds.

3 One of the shortcomings of the Sloane and Reisman framework is that there is no expectational mechanism which rationalizes the ex ante formation of the discount rate.

B Lerner and Carleton have also tried to integrate the investment and financing decisions of the firm into a stock valuation model.

1 Equity values must be based on supply and demand considerations, properly modified to account for the particular characteristics of corporate securities.

2 The general form of this two-equation system contains the following expressions:

(a) A stock valuation equation, with the market price of a security a function of the expected rates of return, retention, interest, and the firm's capital structure.
(b) A model of investment opportunities, defined by the same variables as above and used as a constraint for the product and factor markets.
(c) A constraint for the financial markets, defined in terms of the interest rate and the firm's capital structure.
(d) A set of equilibrium conditions for the expectations of management and stockholders about the rates of return and retention.

3 There are a number of analytical advantages to the Lerner and Carleton model:
(a) The discount rate is separated into the risk-free interest rate and the risk-class specification for the firm.
(b) The investment-opportunity schedule of the firm is specified in terms of its demand and cost functions.
(c) The financial market constraint is specified in terms of the interest rate and the risk exposure of the funds.

C More recent work has focused on the nature of risk dimensions and the generalizations of the valuation model within the time-state-preference framework.

1 This framework relies on the proposition that outcomes of investment decisions can be described by the mutually exclusive and exhaustive future states of the world.
2 Wealth is expressed in terms of real dollars, where the attitudes of investors toward future receipts will determine the relative desirability of these receipts.
3 The only assumption required by this framework is that the investor's indifference curves be concave, to indicate risk aversion; future expectations are implicitly evaluated in the formation of the investor's indifference curves.
4 When the investment horizon is separated into two periods, perhaps "now" and "later," the approach is known as time-state preference.

VI There are a number of explanations for the poor empirical performance of the testable valuation models.

A Some of these models are analytically restricted by unacceptable behavioral assumptions and empirically by the current state of our methodology.

B The quality of the input data may not be compatible or consistent with the structural form of the model.

C The typical equity valuation model is not dynamic enough to allow for imaginative behavior or an error-correcting mechanism.

D The complications of uncertainty do not permit the precise specification of risk.

QUESTIONS FOR SELF-EXAMINATION

True or False

_____ 1 The chartist believes that future share prices can be predicted from their past price movements.

_____ 2 A chartist's prediction will also take into consideration current news releases and the current earnings of the firm.

_____ 3 The economic interpretation of the random-walk theory is founded on the proposition that speculative markets allocate resources efficiently.

_____ 4 The empirical evidence mentioned in the chapter tends to confirm the proposed random nature of security price changes.

_____ 5 Some persistence or dependence of security price changes, however, seems to occur also.

_____ 6 A stock valuation model should integrate the investment and financing decisions of the firm.

_____ 7 One of the advantages of the Sloane and Reisman model is that it separates the discount rate into the risk-free interest rate and the risk-class specification for the firm.

_____ 8 An aavantage of the Lerner and Carleton model is that the investment-opportunity schedule of the firm is specified in terms of its demand and cost functions.

_____ 9 The only assumption required by the time-state-preference approach is the short-run imperfection of capital markets.

_____ 10 The DECP LION framework of Sloane and Reisman permits only the cash-flow hypothesis and equity financing.

Multiple Choice

_____ 1 Which of the following is one of the hypotheses of the theory of random walks?

(a) Investors purchase a security for the expected flow of dividends.
(b) Enough imperfection exists in capital markets to allow for short-term trends.
(c) The market value of a firm is based on its intrinsic value.
(d) Security price changes conform to some probability distribution.

_____ 2 The Sloane and Reisman framework and the Lerner and Carleton framework seem to follow the _____ approach to security valuation.

(a) random-walk
(b) technical
(c) fundamental
(d) none of the above

_____ 3 The Lerner and Carleton two-equation system does not contain which of the following expressions?

(a) A set of equilibrium conditions
(b) A model of investment opportunities
(c) A probability statement of the future states of the world
(d) A stock valuation equation

_____ 4 Essential to the time-state-preference framework of security valuation is the specification of _______

(a) a probability distribution for security price changes.
(b) the investor's indifference curves.
(c) the expected earnings stream of the firm.
(d) the investor's future expectations.

_____ 5 Which of the following is not a reason for the poor empirical performance of the testable valuation models?

(a) Analytical restrictions
(b) Academic prejudices
(c) The complications of uncertainty
(d) The quality of the input data

15 Financial Ratio Analysis

Theme Chapter 15 presents some simple ratios that are typically used in the analysis of financial statements. These ratios are employed as supplementary tools in reaching decisions about a firm's liquidity, profitability, leverage, and coverage positions.

I Financial ratios are simple measures of expected performance based on current data from the firm's financial statements.

A They are static measures that are believed to reflect the firm's ability to pay its obligations as they mature and the firm's efficiency of such important activities as sales and investment.

B Taken by themselves, these static measures cannot tell the investigator much about the current or future position of the firm; however, they can be meaningfully employed in the following ways:

1 By computing a series of specific measures over monthly, quarterly, or yearly intervals, an investigator can obtain a series of snapshots of the firm's behavior over a given horizon.
2 By computing a series of specific measures for comparable firms in an industry, an investigator may be able to delineate the performance of a particular firm as compared with the average performance of other firms in the industry.
3 By computing a time series of specific measures for a number of representative firms in an industry, an investigator may obtain a better picture of the firm's performance within its market environment.

C As several studies have shown, if an appropriate data base is obtained, it is possible to use some of the financial ratios for predictive purposes.

II Financial ratios can generally be classified into four broad categories: liquidity ratios, debt ratios, profitability ratios, and coverage ratios.

A Liquidity ratios are designed to measure the ability of the firm to cover its short-term obligations.

1 The current ratio, current assets/current liabilities, is a popular measure of the overall liquidity of the firm.
(a) Its magnitude is believed to vary directly with the firm's ability to pay its short-term obligations.
(b) It is a rather crude measure, though, in that by lumping together all current assets and all current liabilities, it conceals the different attributes of the individual components.

2 The acid-test, or quick, ratio (current assets less inventories)/current liabilities, is a measure of overall liquidity that attempts to rectify the above criticism of the current ratio.
   (a) By eliminating inventories from total current assets, the quick ratio yields a more homogeneous measure of the firm's liquidity.
   (b) However, it is still a crude measure of liquidity.
3 The average-collection-period ratio (accounts receivable × 365)/annual credit sales, is a more refined measure of specific liquidity that focuses on the average number of calendar days the firm's receivables are outstanding.
4 The receivable-turnover ratio, annual credit sales/accounts receivable, is a measure of the slowness with which receivables are converted into cash.
   (a) From the viewpoint of the outside evaluator, the average-collection-period ratio and the receivables-turnover ratio have a few limitations:
      (i) The credit sales figures may not be easily available; resorting to the figure for net sales, the evaluator may compute a longer average collection period or a smaller receivable turnover ratio than actually exists.
      (ii) Since the amount typically employed for accounts receivable refers to the year-end value, these ratios might be distorted because of seasonalities or sales growth during the year.
   (b) The average-collection-period ratio and the receivables-turnover ratio must be judged in light of the credit terms offered by the firm.
      (i) If the average collection period is consistently longer than the stated terms of credit, it signals trouble and the need for higher credit standards.
      (ii) An average collection period that is consistently shorter than the stated terms of credit indicates a restrictive credit policy and the need for a relaxation of the firm's credit standards.
5 The aging of accounts receivable is another measure of the slowness with which accounts receivable are converted into cash.
   (a) First, classify receivables by the proportions billed in each of the previous months.
   (b) Then by comparing the firm's credit terms with the aging of accounts receivable, one can determine whether collection is excessively slow or fast.
6 The aging-of-accounts-payable ratio (accounts payable × 365)/purchase of raw materials, is designed to measure the slowness of conversion of the firm's accounts payable into cash.
7 The payable-turnover ratio, annual purchases/accounts payable, is another measure of the rate of payables conversion.
8 The inventory-turnover ratio, cost of goods sold/average inventory, is a measure of the degree of liquidity associated with the firm's inventories.
   (a) This ratio actually measures the speed with which inventories are converted through sales into receivables and is believed to vary directly with the efficiency of inventory management.
   (b) Special care must be taken to interpret this ratio within the conditions in the industry and the particular characteristics of the firm.
9 The basic defensive interval, total defensive assets/projected daily operating expenditures, is another measure of the overall liquidity of the firm.
   (a) Total defensive assets are equal to the sum of cash, marketable securities, notes receivable, and accounts receivable; projected daily operating expenditures are equal to the sum of cost of goods sold, selling expenses, and general and administrative expenses, all divided by 365.
   (b) The basic defensive interval is designed to measure the number of days that the firm can operate on its current liquid assets, excluding inventories, without any cash inflows.

B Debt or leverage ratios are designed to reflect the extent to which the firm's assets have been financed by debt.

1 The debt ratio, total debt/total assets, is a crude measure designed to highlight the percentage of total assets to which creditors of all kinds have a claim.

2 The debt-to-net-worth or debt-to-equity ratio, total debt/net worth, is a popular measure designed to reflect the firm's capital structure.
   (a) Ordinarily, total debt includes current liabilities, and net worth excludes treasury stock.
   (b) However, depending upon its intended use, this ratio has several variations.

3 The long-term-debt-to-total-capitalization ratio, long-term debt/total capitalization, is a measure that reflects the relative importance of long-term debt in the firm's capital structure.

C Profitability ratios are typically computed with reference to either sales or investment.

1 Profitability in relation to sales:
   (a) The gross-profit-margin ratio (sales less cost of goods sold)/sales, is a measure designed to reflect the relative operating efficiency of the firm and its pricing policies.
   (b) The net-profit-margin ratio, earnings after taxes/sales, is a more refined measure of the ratio above.

2 Profitability in relation to investment:
   (a) The rate of return on common stock (book value), (earnings after taxes less dividend on preferred stock)/(net worth less par value of preferred stock), indicates the earnings power of a stockholder's investment.
   (b) The return-on-assets ratio, earnings after taxes/total tangible assets, is a more general measure of investment profitability.
   (c) The net-operating-earnings rate of return, earnings before interest and taxes/total tangible assets, is a refinement of the return on assets ratio that abstracts from the firm's methods of financing.
   (d) The turnover ratio, sales/total tangible assets, is a measure of the efficiency with which the firm utilizes its resources.
   (e) The earnings-power or return-on-assets ratio, earnings after taxes/total tangible assets, is an attempt to improve on the shortcomings of the net-profit-margin ratio and the turnover ratio.
      (i) The former overlooks the utilization of assets, and the latter overlooks the profitability on sales.
      (ii) The earnings-power ratio can also be expressed as the product of the net profit margin and the turnover ratios.

D Coverage ratios are designed to judge the firm's ability to pay interest charges on its various debt claims and to repay the principal on these obligations.

1 The times-interest-earned ratio, earnings before interest and taxes/interest charges, is a measure of the extent to which the firm's earnings can decrease before it is unable to meet its obligations.

2 The fixed-charge-coverage ratio, income available for covering fixed charges/fixed charges, is a more inclusive measure of the firm's fixed obligations than the times-interest-earned ratio.

3 The total-coverage ratio, earnings before interest and taxes $\{$interest charges + principal payments $[1/(1 - T)]\}$, is a general measure of the firm's ability to meet all types of obligations associated with the interest and principal payments to its creditors.
   (a) Interest payments are made before taxes.
   (b) However, since principal payments are made after taxes, it is necessary to adjust a term in this ratio for the tax rate, T.

QUESTIONS FOR SELF-EXAMINATION

True or False

____ 1 When using financial ratios, one must take care to use meaningful data and to make comparative analyses with firms of approximately similar attributes.

____ 2 The aging of accounts payable and the payable-turnover ratios suffer from the same types of limitations as the average-collection-period and the receivable-turnover ratios.

____ 3 A financial ratio is a dynamic measure of the desirability of a firm as an investment.

____ 4 The current ratio is a measure of the short-term profitability of the firm.

____ 5 The inventory-turnover ratio is a measure of the degree of liquidity associated with the firm's inventories.

____ 6 If the average collection period is consistently longer than the stated terms of credit, it indicates the need for a relaxation of the firm's credit standards.

____ 7 The basic defensive interval is designed to measure the number of days that the firm can operate on its current liquid assets, excluding inventories, without any cash inflows.

____ 8 A financial ratio is a good indicator of the current or future position of the firm.

____ 9 The total-coverage ratio is a general measure of the firm's ability to meet all types of obligations associated with the interest and principal payments to its creditors.

____ 10 Liquidity ratios are all measures of asset convertibility.

Multiple Choice

____ 1 ____ ratios are designed to measure the ability of the firm to cover its short-term obligations.
- (a) Liquidity
- (b) Debt
- (c) Profitability
- (d) Coverage

____ 2 By eliminating inventories from total current assets, the ____ yields a more homogeneous measure of the firm's liquidity than the current ratio.
- (a) turnover ratio
- (b) acid-test ratio
- (c) payable-turnover ratio
- (d) average-collection-period ratio

____ 3 The ____ is a popular measure designed to reflect the firm's capital structure.
- (a) return-on-assets ratio
- (b) total-coverage ratio
- (c) debt-to-net-worth ratio
- (d) net-profit-margin ratio

____ 4 The ____ is a measure designed to reflect the relative operating efficiency of the firm and its pricing policies.
- (a) return-on-assets ratio
- (b) total-coverage ratio
- (c) average-collection-period ratio
- (d) net-profit-margin ratio

____ 5 If the sales for a firm were $18 million, its turnover ratio were 2.0, and its earnings power ratio were 1.5, then the earnings after taxes for the firm must be ____
- (a) $13.5 million.
- (b) $9 million.
- (c) $12 million.
- (d) $12.75 million.

1 Following are the financial statements of Spray Textile, Inc.:

Spray Textile, Inc., balance sheet, June 30, 1974

Assets		
Current Assets:		
Cash	$ 45,000	
Marketable securities	82,500	
Accounts receivable	165,000	
Inventories	232,500	
Total current assets		$ 525,000
Long-term Assets:		
Land	$468,750	
Building and equipment	356,250	825,000
Total assets		$1,350,000
Liabilities and Stockholders Equity		
Current Liabilities:		
Accounts payable	$ 60,000	
Notes payable	105,000	
Accruals	22,500	
Total current liabilities		$ 187,500
Long-term Liabilities:		
Mortgage note payable	$262,500	
Bonds payable	150,000	412,500
Total liabilities		$ 600,000
Stockholders Equity:		
Capital stock	$450,000	
Retained earnings	300,000	
Total stockholders equity		750,000
Total liabilities and stockholders equity		$1,350,000

Spray Textile, Inc., income statement, for year ended June 30, 1974

Net Sales		$2,409,000
Cost of goods sold		2,092,500
Gross Profit		$ 316,500
Selling expenses	$99,000	
General and administrative expenses	52,500	
Total Operating Expenses		151,500
Net earnings from operations		$ 165,000
Interest expense		30,000
Net earnings before taxes		$ 135,000
Federal income taxes (40%)		54,000
Net earnings after taxes		$ 81,000

Compute the financial ratios listed below in the solution.

Solution

Liquidity ratios:

Current ratio $\dfrac{\$525{,}000}{\$187{,}500} = 2.80$

Acid-test, or quick, ratio $\dfrac{(\$525{,}000 - \$232{,}500)}{\$187{,}500} = 1.56$

Average-collection-period ratio $\dfrac{(\$165{,}000 \times 365)}{\$2{,}409{,}000} = 25$ days

Receivable-turnover ratio $\dfrac{\$2{,}409{,}000}{\$165{,}000} = 14.6$ times

Inventory-turnover ratio $\dfrac{\$2{,}092{,}500}{\$232{,}500} = 9$ times

Basic defensive interval $\dfrac{\$45{,}000 + \$82{,}500 + \$165{,}000}{(\$2{,}092{,}500 + \$99{,}000 + \$52{,}500)/365} = \dfrac{292{,}500}{6{,}148} = 47.58$ days

Debt ratios:

Debt ratio $\dfrac{\$600{,}000}{\$1{,}350{,}000} = 44.44\%$

Debt-to-equity ratio $\dfrac{\$600{,}000}{\$750{,}000} = 80.0\%$

Profitability ratios:

Gross-profit-margin ratio $\dfrac{\$316{,}500}{\$2{,}409{,}000} = 13.14\%$

Net-profit-margin ratio $\dfrac{\$81{,}000}{\$2{,}409{,}000} = 3.36\%$

Rate of return on common stock $\dfrac{\$81{,}000}{\$750{,}000} = 10.8\%$

Return-on-assets ratio or earnings power $\dfrac{\$81{,}000}{\$1{,}350{,}000} = 6.0\%$

Turnover ratio $\dfrac{\$2{,}409{,}000}{\$1{,}350{,}000} = 1.78$ times

Coverage ratio:

Times-interest-earned ratio $\dfrac{(\$135{,}000 + \$30{,}000)}{\$30{,}000} = 5.5$ times

2 The Greater Supply Company has annual sales of \$4.1 million. This sales level produced a gross-profit-margin ratio, net-profit-margin ratio, and return-on-assets ratio of 10%, 6%, and 8%, respectively. Determine for Greater Supply their (a) cost of goods sold, (b) earnings after taxes, (c) total tangible assets, and (d) turnover ratio.

Solution

(a) Gross-profit-margin ratio = (sales − cost of goods sold)/sales

Cost of goods sold = sales − sales × gross-profit-margin ratio
= \$4,100,000 − \$4,100,000 × .10
= \$4,100,000 − \$410,000
= \$3,690,000

(b) Earnings after taxes = net-profit-margin ratio × sales
$= .06 \times \$4{,}100{,}000$
$= \$246{,}000$

(c) Total tangible assets = earnings after taxes/return-on-assets ratio

$$= \frac{\$246{,}000}{.08}$$

$= \$3{,}075{,}000$

(d) Turnover ratio = sales/total tangible assets

$$= \frac{\$4{,}100{,}000}{\$3{,}075{,}000}$$

$= 1.33$

3 Determine the net worth of a firm with the following financial characteristics: debt-to-equity ratio of 33 1/3%, debt ratio of 25%, and total assets of $5,728,000.

Solution

$$\text{Debt ratio} = \frac{\text{total debt}}{\text{total assets}}$$

Total debt = debt ratio × total assets
$= .25 \times \$5{,}728{,}000$
$= \$1{,}432{,}000$

Debt-to-equity ratio = total debt/net worth

Net worth = total debt/debt-to-equity ratio
$= \$1{,}432{,}000/(1/3)$
$= \$4{,}296{,}000$

4 The Sandy Company has total current assets of $341,000, inventories of $200,000, and total current liabilities of $128,000. Subsequently, the company pays $35,000 in cash to reduce their accounts payable. Compute the company's current and quick ratios before and after the $35,000 transaction.

Solution

Before:

$$\text{Current ratio} = \frac{\$341{,}000}{\$128{,}000} = 2.66$$

$$\text{Quick ratio} = \frac{(\$341{,}000 - \$200{,}000)}{\$128{,}000} = 1.10$$

After:

New current assets = $341,000 − $35,000 = $306,000

New current liabilities = $128,000 − $35,000 = $93,000

$$\text{Current ratio} = \frac{\$306{,}000}{\$93{,}000} = 3.29$$

$$\text{Quick ratio} = \frac{(\$306{,}000 - \$200{,}000)}{\$93{,}000} = 1.14$$

5 The financial statements of Evaluation Corporation are

Evaluation Corporation, balance sheet, September 30, 1974

Assets		
Current Assets:		
Cash	$ 60,000	
Marketable securities	110,000	
Accounts receivable	220,000	
Inventories	310,000	
Total current assets		$ 700,000
Long-term Assets:		
Land	$625,000	
Building and Equipment	475,000	1,100,000
Total assets		$1,800,000
Liabilities and Stockholders Equity		
Current Liabilities:		
Accounts payable	$ 80,000	
Notes payable	140,000	
Accruals	30,000	
Total current liabilities		$ 250,000
Long-term Liabilities:		
Mortgage note payable	$350,000	
Bonds payable	200,000	550,000
Total liabilities		$ 800,000
Stockholders Equity:		
Capital stock	$600,000	
Retained earnings	400,000	
Total stockholders equity		1,000,000
Total liabilities and stockholders equity		$1,800,000

Evaluation Corporation, income statement, for year ended September 30, 1974

Net Sales		$3,212,000
Cost of goods sold		2,790,000
Gross Profit		$ 422,000
Selling expenses	$132,000	
General and administrative expenses	70,000	
Total operating expenses		202,000
Net earnings from operations		$ 220,000
Interest expense		40,000
Net earnings before taxes		$ 180,000
Federal income taxes (40%)		72,000
Net earnings after taxes		$ 108,000

Determine the financial ratios listed below.

Solution

Current ratio =

Quick ratio =

Average-collection-period ratio =

Receivable-turnover ratio =

Inventory-turnover ratio =

Debt ratio =

Debt-to-equity ratio =

Gross-profit-margin ratio =

Net-profit-margin ratio =

Rate of return on common stock =

Return-on-assets ratio or earnings power =

Turnover ratio =

Times-interest-earned ratio =

6 Mr. Wilson is analyzing the Tip-Top Company as a potential investment. Information he has acquired indicates that with sales of $3.5 million, Tip-Top had a 5% net profit margin and returned 8% on assets. For further analysis, Mr. Wilson needs the company's total tangible assets and turnover ratio. Supply him with these figures.

Solution

7 The Balance Statement of Tip-Top Company in Problem 6 reveals a 20% debt ratio. Employing this information with that in the problem, determine the rate of return to the holders of Tip-Top common stock. (Assume no preferred stock.)

Solution

16 Mathematical Programming and Financial Decisions

Theme Chapter 16 discusses a family of techniques for determining the optimal program of interdependent, constrained activities — mathematical programming.

I Fractional or linear programming requires that an objective function be maximized or minimized, subject to a set of contraints. It permits fractional solution values.

A It assumes that the functional relationships within a problem are linear and that the parameters of the problem are known with certainty.

B The linear programming technique is outlined below.

1 Accurately specify all that is relevant to the solution of the problem.
(a) The constraints of the problem should be expressed as inequalities.
(b) The objective function, a schedule that relates the variable to be optimized to the decision variables, should be expressed as an equality.
2 Optimize the value of the objective function without violating any of the constraints.

C A graphic solution can be obtained if the problem contains only two variables and a few constraints.

1 Convert the inequalities to equalities.
2 Graph the equalities on a Cartesian plane. Since the equalities are really inequalities, the resultant lines will form the upper boundary of a maximization problem or the lower boundary of a minimization problem.
3 Establish nonnegativity constraints since meaningful solution values cannot be less than zero.
4 The combination of the problem constraints and the nonnegativity constraints determines the area of feasible solutions. Although any point on or within this region is a feasible solution, the optimal solution can be found only at an intersection or corner point of the constraint lines.
5 Develop a system of isoquant (equal quantity) lines by setting the objective function equal to ascending values for a maximization problem or descending values for a minimization problem.
(a) An isoquant line is the locus of points such that any combination of the two variables along this line will give the same value of the objective function.
(b) For any given objective function, all isoquant lines have the same slope; i.e., they are all parallel.
(c) The farther away from the origin that an isoquant line lies, the larger its value.
6 Since the point of optimization will always lie on the boundary of the feasible region, choose the boundary point that just touches the largest isoquant line for a maximization problem or the smallest isoquant line for a minimization problem.

(a) The optimum isoquant line may be tangent to a corner point.
(b) The optimum isoquant line may lie on a boundary (constraint) line, in which case all the points on this segment are optimum, including the two corner points.

D Most linear programming problems contain more than three variables and, as a consequence, can only be solved algebraically.

E The simplex method, an iterative process that proceeds in a finite number of steps to an optimum solution, may be used to solve algebraically a linear programming problem. Its four basic steps are

1 Select a corner of the feasible set as a starting point.
2 Choose an edge through this corner point such that as one moves along it, the value of the objective function increases for a maximization problem or decreases for a minimization problem.
3 Proceed along this edge to the next corner point.
4 Repeat steps 2 and 3 until one cannot increase (decrease) the value of the objective function by a movement along a boundary of the feasible set; this last corner point is an optimum solution.

F Every linear programming problem formulated as a maximization problem has associated with it a corresponding minimization formulation; the converse is also true.

1 The original formulation is called the primal and the corresponding formulation is called the dual.
2 A formal, one-to-one correspondence exists between every term of the primal and every term of the dual.
   (a) For example, each variable in the objective function of the dual is associated with a right-hand side value of each of the problem constraints in the primal.
   (b) These dual variables, also called shadow prices, represent the opportunity costs associated with the constraints of the primal problem.
   (c) The shadow price associated with a specific constraint shows how much more the objective function can be optimized if the constraint is relaxed by one unit.

II Integer programming is essentially linear programming with integer solution values.

A An integer programming formulation may result from two restrictions that are often attached to a capital-budgeting problem.

1 A project must be either accepted or rejected.
2 A project can be accepted or rejected only once.

B When the only meaningful solution values to a problem are 0 or 1 (reject or accept), an integer-programming formulation is appropriate; the restricted variables are often called zero-one variables.

C Pure integer programming requires that all the variables have integer solutions; mixed integer programming formulations require that only some of the variables have integer solutions.

D Although integer programming methods are numerous, specialized, and require a great degree of discretion for their successful application, they avoid two serious complications of ordinary linear programming:

1 Rounding up to an integer may cause the optimum solution to become infeasible.
2 Rounding down to an integer may cause the optimum solution to become less than optimum.

E The real importance of integer programming derives from its ability to handle concisely almost any combinatorial problem, such as portfolio selection.

III Dynamic programming is used to handle problems characterized by sequential, interrelated decisions.

A For this type of problem, one is interested in finding an optimal policy or a particular sequence of decisions that will optimize the objective function for the entire decision horizon.

B Dynamic programming utilizes the simultaneous application of two concepts: recursive optimality and the summarization of information in terms of a state variable.

1 Recursive optimality allows the decision maker to divide a problem into suitable subproblems and to find the optimal policy by proceeding from the last stage to the first in a backward (recursive) fashion.
2 The concept of a state variable refers to the current information at each stage or subproblem being contained in a variable.

C If a problem cannot be described by a small number of states, then dynamic programming loses much of its operational usefulness.

D The dynamic programming technique is outlined below.

1 Divide the original problem into a number of subproblems or stages, and use state variables to define the present situation at each stage.
2 Find the optimal decision rule for each state of the last subproblem and proceed backward to the first subproblem. An optimal decision rule specifies a particular decision as a function of the stage and a state variable.
3 Record the payoff from each stage. An optimal policy delineates a set of optimal decision rules that guide one throughout all the stages of a problem.

IV Several special programming methods are mentioned below.

Decomposition programming is used for the solution of large-scale problems that can be separated into a number of subproblems which possess some common rows or variables.

B Nonlinear programming is used for the solution of problems that involve a nonlinear objective function, nonlinear constraints, or both.

C Stochastic programming is used for the solution of nonlinear programming problems that contain both inequality constraints and random variables.

D Goal programming is a variation of linear programming that is used to solve problems which are characterized by multiple goals.

1 It allows one to include multiple goals in his objective function and to assign special priorities by a weighting system.
2 In a goal programming situation, one compromises an optimal solution to a single goal for a satisfactory solution to multiple goals.

V Another important consideration of mathematical programming revolves about sensitivity analysis or parametric programming.

A Sensitivity or postoptimality analysis is a generalized framework for testing the robustness of a model by relaxing some of the assumptions and observing the behavior of the system under the new conditions.

B Parametric programming is a standard procedure for testing the robustness of the original model by changing coefficients in the objective function or by changing the right-hand side of the inequality constraints.

QUESTIONS FOR SELF-EXAMINATION

True or False

_____ 1 In linear programming, the objective function may contain multiple goals, all of which are optimized.

_____ 2 Although it may not be unique, an optimum solution to a solvable linear programming problem can always be found at a corner point of the feasible region.

_____ 3 The shadow price associated with a specific constraint shows how much more the objective function can be optimized if the constraint is relaxed by one unit.

_____ 4 Recursive optimality refers to the optimal information at each stage of a problem.

_____ 5 In dynamic programming, an optimal decision rule specifies a particular decision as a function of the stage and a state variable.

_____ 6 Parametric programming is used for the solution of problems that involve nonlinear functions.

_____ 7 In goal programming, one compromises an optimal solution to a single goal for a satisfactory solution to multiple goals.

_____ 8 Linear programming assumes that the functional relationships within a problem are linear and that the parameters of the problem are known with certainty.

_____ 9 Sensitivity analysis may give one some insight into the sensitivity of a model to a misspecification of a constraint or an incorrect estimate of an input parameter.

_____ 10 Integer programming avoids the potential problems associated with the rounding off of a fractional solution.

Multiple Choice

_____ 1 In a graphic solution to a linear programming problem that seeks the maximization of the objective function, the plotted inequalities will form the _____
(a) isoquant lines.
(b) upper boundary.
(c) lower boundary.
(d) none of the above.

_____ 2 When the only meaningful solution values to a problem are 0 or 1, signifying, for example, reject or accept, respectively, a _____ formulation is appropriate.
(a) dynamic programming
(b) stochastic programming
(c) integer programming
(d) goal programming

_____ 3 Dynamic programming is used to handle problems characterized by _____
(a) nonlinear functions.
(b) sequential, interrelated decisions.
(c) common rows or variables.
(d) random variables.

_____ 4 _____ would probably be used to solve a problem with a quadratic objective function.
(a) Nonlinear programming
(b) Goal programming
(c) Fractional programming
(d) Decomposition programming

_____ 5 The real importance of integer programming derives from its ability to _____
(a) provide integer solutions.
(b) handle pure or mixed formulations.
(c) satisfy multiple goals.
(d) handle combinatorial problems concisely.

PROBLEMS FOR PRACTICE

1 Three new drill press models are being considered by the Lion Drill Company as additions to their retail line. An analysis of the associated costs and benefits yielded the following schedule on a per unit basis:

Model	*NPV of Benefits*	*PV of Costs*
A	$ 75	$40
B	85	50
C	110	70

The present value of the capital-budget constraint is $3,500. One concern of Lion Drill is the floor space requirements for in-process and final inventory of the drill presses. By rearranging current storage, a maximum of 1,500 square feet of floor space can be allocated to the new drill presses. The three models, A, B, and C, will use 3.0, 2.5, and 3.4 square feet of space per unit. Formulate this problem in a linear programming framework to determine the number of units of each model for Lion Drill to produce.

Solution

Decision variables:

X_j = number of units of jth model to produce where $j = A, B, C$

Objective function:

Maximize: NPV = $75X_A + 85X_B + 110X_C$

Constraints:

Subject to:

$40X_A + 50X_B + 70X_C \leqslant 3{,}500$ cost constraint

$3.0X_A + 2.5X_B + 3.4X_C \leqslant 1{,}500$ floor space constraint

$X_A \geqslant 0 \quad X_B \geqslant 0 \quad X_C \geqslant 0$ nonnegativity constraints

2 The Equipment Supply Company has determined that their cash needs during the next two months from external sources are $90,000 in the first month and $120,000 in the second month. They have three alternative sources for the funds. There is a line of credit with their bank at .75% interest per month with a loan limit of $110,000. At the current time, none of available credit is in use. Any funds obtained through the line of credit will not be repaid during the next two months. The bank will also loan funds to the company on a term basis at .75% interest per month but with a 15% compensating balance requirement. In addition, the company may obtain needed cash through the commercial paper market at an interest rate of .625% per month. The commercial paper issued has a 30-day maturity; thus any amount obtained in the first month must be refinanced at the beginning of the second month. To maintain friendly relations with their banker, Equipment Supply has maintained a policy of limiting their reliance on the commercial paper market to a maximum of half their external cash requirements. All borrowing is accomplished at the beginning of the month. Equipment Supply's objective is to minimize

interest costs. Formulate this problem in a linear programming framework to determine the amount of funds obtained from each source at the beginning of each month.

Solution

Decision variables:

X_i = funds borrowed from bank line of credit for period i

Y_i = funds borrowed with commercial paper for period i

Z_i = funds borrowed with bank term loan for period i

C_i = cash needs for period i

i = period 1, 2

Objective function:

$$\text{Minimize: } .0075X_1 + .0075(X_1 + X_2) + .00625Y_1 + .00625Y_2 + .0075Z_1 + .0075(Z_1 + Z_2)$$

Constraints:

Subject to:

$X_1 \leqslant 110{,}000$	line of credit maximum, $i = 1$
$X_1 + X_2 \leqslant 110{,}000$	line of credit maximum, $i = 2$
$X_1 + Z_1 - Y_1 \geqslant 0$	commercial paper limit, $i = 1$
$X_1 + X_2 + Z_1 + Z_2 - Y_2 \geqslant 0$	commercial paper limit, $i = 2$
$X_1 + Y_1 + .85Z_1 \geqslant 90{,}000$	cash needs requirements, $i = 1$
$X_2 + Y_2 - Y_1 + .85Z_2 \geqslant 120{,}000$	cash needs requirements, $i = 2$
$X_i \geqslant 0 \quad Y_i \geqslant 0 \quad Z_i \geqslant 0$	nonnegativity constraints

17 Techniques for Multiple-Project Selection

Theme Chapter 17 reformulates the investment decision within the framework of multiproject-single-period choices. This formulation, known as portfolio selection, has implications for the entire range of investment decisions.

I The problem of portfolio selection derives from the intercorrelations among the flows of the individual assets included in an investor's set.

A The investor's goal of an efficient portfolio can be stated in either of two ways:

1 Combine a group of assets such that for a given level of risk, one maximizes his return.
2 Combine a group of assets such that for a given level of return, one minimizes his risk.

B Given some set of previously selected assets and an initial cash endowment, one uses portfolio-selection techniques to decide on the various proportions of his endowment that will be invested in each asset.

C Because of our emphasis on financial assets, a portfolio will be defined as the composite set of ownership rights to financial assets in which the investor has invested his funds.

D Since one's portfolio is the end result of his cumulative investment decisions, it represents his attitudes and inclinations for certain types of financial assets, risk, and return.

1 A portfolio is a unique arrangement of assets designed to satisfy the needs of the owner.
2 For example, liquid assets may be held for their ease of convertibility into cash, their expected return, or, in the case of cash, for their transactional convenience.

E There are three steps in the selection of a portfolio:

1 The preselection of eligible financial instruments from which one can derive potential subsets.
2 The estimation of the risk-return characteristics of each of the eligible securities.
3 The proportional allocation of the investor's funds among the securities such that the portfolio risk is minimized, subject to a prespecified expected return.

F Portfolio selection involves two behavioral assumptions:

1 An investor prefers higher returns to lower returns, for any given level of risk.
2 An investor prefers certain returns to uncertain returns, for any given level of return.

II Diversification is the allocation of investment funds among several eligible securities in order to avoid an unsuccessful single investment.

A Diversification helps one construct a risk-averting portfolio.

1 Although it does not reduce the expected return from a portfolio, it does reduce the instability of expected returns.
2 Diversification decreases the probability of lower than expected returns, as well as the probability of higher than expected returns.

B There are two general reasons for the instability of investment returns:

1 Internal causes, such as erratic or generally irrational behavior by a firm's management.
2 External causes, which include the effects of the following factors on expected returns:
(a) Long-term industry trends affect the growth, safety, and desirability of investments in the industry.
(b) Cyclical business fluctuations affect the price of securities.
(c) Monetary inflation affects the real value of one's investments and their return.
(d) Interest-rate risk affects fixed-income securities through the risk associated with market price fluctuations and the risk associated with income fluctuations.

C The expected return and the stability of expected returns from a portfolio are closely related to the expected return and the stability of expected returns from its component securities.

1 The expected return from a portfolio is the weighted average of the expected return from each security in the portfolio.
2 The stability of portfolio returns is usually measured by the standard deviation of the probable returns to the portfolio.

D The standard deviation of portfolio returns is determined by the standard deviation of returns from each security, the correlation between the returns from each pair of securities, and the amount invested in each security.

1 The correlation coefficient, ρ_{ij}, measures the amount of variability in the returns from security i that is associated with the variability in the returns from security j. It may assume any value from -1 to $+1$.
(a) Perfect positive correlation, $\rho_{ij} = 1$, means that the returns from one security will move in exact accordance with the returns from the other security.
(b) Perfect negative correlation, $\rho_{ij} = -1$, means that the returns from one security will move by the same proportion but in the opposite direction to the returns from the other security.
(c) Zero correlation, $\rho_{ij} = 0$, means that there is no relation between the returns from two securities.
2 In general, the greater the correlation between the returns from portfolio securities, the greater the standard deviation of the portfolio, *ceteris paribus*.

III The computation of the summary statistical measures for a portfolio is described below.

A The expected return from a portfolio, E_p, is computed as follows:

$$E_p = \sum_{i=1}^{n} X_i E_i$$

where n = number of securities in the portfolio
X_i = proportion of total portfolio funds invested in ith security
E_i = expected rate of return from ith security

1 E_i is the mean of the probability distribution of expected returns from the ith security.

2 $$E_i = \sum_{i=1}^{n} P_i 0_i$$

where n = number of outcomes
P_i = probability of occurrence of ith outcome
0_i = ith outcome

B The standard deviation of portfolio returns is computed as follows:

$$\sigma_p = \sqrt{\sum_{i=1}^{n} \sum_{j=1}^{n} X_i X_j C_{ij}}$$

where n = number of securities in portfolio
X_i, X_j = proportions of total portfolio fund invested in ith and jth securities, respectively
C_{ij} = covariance between returns from ith and jth securities

1 The covariance between the returns from security i and security j is computed as follows:

$$C_{ij} = \rho_{ij}\sigma_i\sigma_j$$

where ρ_{ij} = correlation coefficient between returns from security i and security j
σ_i, σ_j = standard deviations of probability distribution of expected returns from security i and security j, respectively

2 The standard deviation of security i can be computed as follows:

$$\sigma_i = \sqrt{\sum_{i=1}^{n} P_i(0_i - E_i)^2}$$

where the variables are as defined in section III A 2.

IV The Markowitz full-covariance model.

A If one made every possible, proportional combination of eligible securities and then plotted for each of these combinations its variance on the y axis and its mean on the x axis, the result would be the mean-variance diversification area (feasible set).

B The efficient frontier or locus of efficient combinations is a segment on the perimeter of this area such that no other combination yields lower risk (variance) for a given return or a higher return for a given level of risk.

C The optimal portfolio is determined by the utility function of the investor; i.e., given the risk-return preferences of an investor, his optimum portfolio is located at the point of tangency between his highest utility curve and the efficient frontier.

D A serious limitation of this model is the large number of estimates needed to define an efficient portfolio.

V Sharpe's single-index model.

A Sharpe developed a model that greatly reduces the number of computations needed to characterize a portfolio.

B His model specifies the contribution of each security to the portfolio return as the sum of two components:

1 An investment in the basic characteristics of the individual asset.
2 An investment in some relevant market index.

C A few comments on the Sharpe model are necessary.

1 The market index used need not be confined to any one indicator of general economic activity.
2 The relationship between the performance of a security and the relevant index need not be assumed linear.
3 The actual probability distribution of index changes need not be assumed to have equal variance at different levels of the index.

D Sharpe's model ultimately reduces to an index-portfolio return and an index-portfolio variance:

1 $E_p = \sum_{i=1}^{n+1} X_i a_i$

where E_p = index-portfolio return
X_i = proportion of total portfolio fund invested in security i
a_i = a parameter of model

2 $\sigma_p^2 = \sum_{i=1}^{n+1} X_i^2 Z_i$

where σ_p^2 = index-portfolio variance
Z_i = variance of random variable term in model

E The contribution of Sharpe's model is that it reduces the time and costs in generating an efficient portfolio by reducing the number of inputs and the computational complexity of a portfolio selection model.

F Some considerations of Sharpe's index model are

1 In linking an individual security's return to a general market index, some of the important relationships among securities become lost.
2 The index employed may not be general or unique.

G In partial answer to the above considerations, multi-index models have been developed to verify the marginal improvement in a portfolio as one increases the number of indices.

VI If one defines the expected returns from a project as a random variable, then one can use the generalized framework of portfolio selection for capital-budgeting decisions.

A The following assumptions are basic to the utilization of this method of analysis:

1 A consistently reliable relationship exists between the risk associated with an investment and the risk deriving from the overall operations of the firm.
2 A consistently reliable model of security valuation exists.
3 A portfolio-selection procedure exists that will maximize the market value of the firm.

B Quirin's method of choosing risky investments suggests that the acceptance of a project be based on its marginal risk contribution to the overall riskiness of the firm.

1 All projects that increase or maintain the net present value of the firm should be tentatively accepted.
2 The final selection will include those projects that contribute the largest increment to the net present value of the firm.

QUESTIONS FOR SELF-EXAMINATION

True or False

_____ 1 A portfolio is a unique arrangement of assets designed to satisfy the needs of the investor.

_____ 2 Diversification is used to increase the expected returns from a portfolio.

_____ 3 The correlation coefficient measures the proportion of the expected return from a security which is associated with that of another security.

_____ 4 The greater the correlation between the returns from portfolio securities, the greater the standard deviation of the portfolio, *ceteris paribus.*

_____ 5 In the Markowitz model, the optimal portfolio lies on the efficient frontier of the mean-variance diversification area.

_____ 6 Sharpe's model improved on the Markowitz scheme by reducing the number of inputs and the computational complexity of a portfolio-selection model.

_____ 7 Monetary inflation affects the growth and safety of investments in an industry.

_____ 8 The expected return from a portfolio is the weighted average of the expected returns from each security in the portfolio.

_____ 9 Sharpe's model has been improved upon by an increase in the number of summary statistics of the portfolio.

_____ 10 Quirin's method is based on the marginal risk contribution of a project to the overall riskiness of the firm.

Multiple Choice

_____ 1 The problem of portfolio selection derives from _______

(a) the uncertainty of cash flows.
(b) the preferences of the investor.
(c) the investor's aversion to risk.
(d) the intercorrelations among the flows of assets.

_____ 2 Portfolio selection begins with the _______

(a) preselection of eligible financial instruments.
(b) proportional allocation of the funds for investment.
(c) estimation of risk-return characteristics.
(d) specification of the investor's utility function.

_____ 3 Diversification enables one to _______

(a) avoid risk.
(b) reduce uncertainty.
(c) increase expected returns.
(d) reduce the instability of expected returns.

_____ 4 The standard deviation of portfolio returns is not determined by which one of the following?

(a) The standard deviation of individual security returns
(b) The amount invested in each security
(c) The range of security returns
(d) The correlation between security returns

_____ 5 If the correlation coefficient for two securities is –.6, a \$10 increase in the return from one security would be expected to be associated with a _______ in the return from the other.

(a) \$6 decrease
(b) \$6 increase
(c) \$4 increase
(d) none of the above

PROBLEMS FOR PRACTICE

1 Two securities have the following expectational data:

$E_1 = .12 \qquad \sigma_1 = .15$

$E_2 = .06 \qquad \sigma_2 = .05$

Combine these two securities to form five portfolios with Security 1 comprising 0%, 10%, 50%, 80%, and 100% of the respective portfolios. Calculate the portfolio return and the portfolio standard deviation assuming the following correlations between Security 1 and 2: $\rho_{12} = 1.0$, .5, 0, and –.5.

Solution

X_1	X_2	E_p	σ_p $\rho_{12} = 1.0$	$\rho_{12} = .5$	$\rho_{12} = 0$	$\rho_{12} = -.5$
0	1.0	.060	.050	.050	.050	.050
.1	.9	.066	.060	.054	.047	.040
.5	.5	.090	.100	.090	.079	.066
.8	.2	.108	.130	.125	.120	.115
1.0	.0	.120	.150	.150	.150	.150

Sample calculations of the above figures:

$E_p = X_1 E_1 + X_2 E_2$

$\sigma_p^2 = X_1^2 \sigma_1^2 + X_2^2 \sigma_2^2 + 2X_1 X_2 \rho_{12} \sigma_1 \sigma_2$

For $X_1 = .10$, $\rho_{12} = .5$

$E_p = (.1)(.12) + (.9)(.06) = .066$

$\sigma_p^2 = (.1)^2 (.15)^2 + (.9)^2 (.05)^2 + 2(.1)(.9)(.5)(.15)(.05) = .002925$

$\sigma_p = \sqrt{.002925} = .054$

All the remaining elements of the above table are determined in a similar manner. Note that for $X_1 = .1$ and $X_2 = .9$ and when $\rho_{12} = 0$ or $-.5$, the standard deviation of the portfolio is less than a portfolio containing 100% of Security 2.

2 Mr. Brill and his stockbroker have analyzed three securities for possible investment by Mr. Brill. The expected returns and standard deviations of the securities are

Security	*Return*	*Standard Deviations*
1	.09	.08
2	.12	.14
3	.15	.21

Their analysis also indicated that the correlations between the three securities were $\rho_{12} = .3$, $\rho_{13} = .6$, and $\rho_{23} = .5$. After careful deliberation, Mr. Brill elected to invest 20% of his funds in Security 1, 30% in Security 2, and the remainder in Security 3. Determine the expected return and standard deviation of his portfolio.

Solution

$X_1 = .2$, $X_2 = .3$, $X_3 = .5$

$E_p = (.2)(.09) + (.3)(.12) + (.5)(.15) = .129 = 12.9\%$ return

$$\sigma_p^2 = (.2)^2 (.08)^2 + (.3)^2 (.14)^2 + (.5)^2 (.21)^2 + 2(.2)(.3)(.3)(.08)(.14) + 2(.2)(.5)(.6)(.08)(.21) + 2(.3)(.5)(.14)(.21) = .02428$$

$\sigma_p = \sqrt{.02428} = .1558$

PROBLEMS FOR SELF-EXAMINATION

3 Mr. Gary Blunt's existing portfolio has a current market value of \$40,000. Its expected return is 9% with a standard deviation of .06. With a recent inheritance of \$10,000, Mr. Blunt is planning on adding another security to his portfolio. After a diligent search and careful analysis, he

has narrowed the selection to two securities: the Tacky Gum Company and the Loose Glue Company. Relevant financial characteristics of the two companies are

Company	*Expected Return*	*Standard Deviation*	*Correlation with Existing Portfolio*
Tacky Gum	.14	.12	.15
Loose Glue	.16	.10	.80

Which security do you recommend Mr. Blunt to purchase?

Solution

18 Simulation and Financial Decisions

Theme Simulation involves the use of a (sampling) model to approximate the behavior of a real-world system within an artificial environment. Chapter 18 discusses this technique and provides some insights into its application.

I Simulation should be contrasted with a related technique known as gaming.

A One engages in the simulation of a system in order to observe and analyze its behavior under artificially imposed conditions.

B When conducting a gaming experiment, one is primarily interested in the behavior and learning patterns of the human participants in the game.

II Simulation has generally been utilized to distinguish between two basic research approaches:

A Expository simulation attempts to explain certain dynamic behavioral processes that are common among individuals and organizations.

B Evaluative simulation is concerned with the evaluation of certain alternative courses of action and their possible effects on the behavior of the system or its individual members.

III The taxonomy of simulation.

A Simulation can be classified into four types:

1 Descriptive simulation, which attempts to describe a system with the precision and detail necessary to enable the investigator to predict the future states of the system.
2 Quasirealistic simulation, which introduces certain reasonable assumptions into a specific system in order to study its behavior under these modifications.
3 Normative simulation, which is conducted in order to design systems that achieve certain organizational objectives.
4 Interactive simulation, which attempts to train people to function better under specified organizational and market environments. However, to be consistent with the dichotomy of section I, this technique is best viewed as a gaming method.

B Simulation categories converge into four uses:

1 Monte Carlo methods
2 Tactical simulation
3 Exploratory or strategic simulation
4 Artificial intelligence

IV Listed are the six steps in model construction and decision making:

A Observe the system and formulate the problem in precise terms, so that it can eventually be formulated symbolically.

B Specify and construct an analytical model to explain the behavior of the system.

C Use mathematical deduction methods to predict the behavior of the system, under specified values of the variables.

D Test the validity of the model and solutions derived from it.

E Specify the controls on the range of model solutions.

F Implement the model in real-life situations.

V The methodological base of simulation experiments is described below.

A A simulation experiment on the behavior of a system may serve as an acceptable, or as the only possible, substitute for any of the above steps.

1 A step may be impossible to follow due to a lack of historical data or missing observations.
2 A problem may be so unique that it requires the formulation of subjective expectations about future outcomes.

B Simulated observations may be used as substitutes for the missing observations and may enable the analyst to construct, manipulate, and test the model.

C The closer the approximation of a model is to reality, *ceteris paribus*, the more difficult it is to obtain analytical solutions.

1 It is this specific difficulty that highlights the importance of computer simulation.
2 Since numerical analysis techniques are time consuming and expensive, one may choose the option of performing a simulation experiment.

VI Simulation is also applicable to capital-budgeting decisions.

A One approach, based on probabilistic concepts, attempts to assess the uncertainty of future investments and then transform this uncertainty into measurable risk.

B Another approach attempts to assess the internal and external constraints on the investment decisions of the firm. This approach is usually handled by one of three mathematical programming techniques:

1 Linear programming under uncertainty, which divides the problem into two stages — the selection of variable values based on the observation of random variables and the subsequent calculation of the optimum values for the decision variables.
2 Stochastic linear programming, which involves the attainment of repeated solutions in order to obtain a distribution of the outcomes.
3 Chance-constraint programming, which involves the maximization of the expected value of a function, subject to probabilistic constraints.

VII Sensitivity analysis is conducted to ascertain the range of variation in the input parameter values that will permit the stability of output values and retain the model's basic composition.

A It is another way of dealing with uncertainty and is usually combined with some other deterministic or stochastic technique to strengthen the investigator's confidence in the precision of his results.

B Sensitivity analysis is often used when the experimenter is unable to determine precisely the factors necessary for his analysis or to pinpoint the specific factors to which the model is sensitive.

C To apply sensitivity analysis fruitfully and economically, one must be thoroughly familiar with his model, its strategic variables, and their underlying distributions.

QUESTIONS FOR SELF-EXAMINATION

True or False

_____ 1 Expository simulation is a research approach that is concerned with the explanation of alternative courses of action.

_____ 2 Descriptive simulation attempts to design systems that achieve certain organizational objectives.

_____ 3 Quasirealistic simulation is used to study the behavior of a system under modified conditions.

_____ 4 A simulation experiment may serve as an acceptable or as the only possible substitute for a step in the construction of a model.

_____ 5 Sensitivity analysis is conducted to ascertain the range of variation in the input parameters that will maintain the present solution values.

Multiple Choice

_____ 1 Which of the following words or phrases is least likely to be associated with simulation?
(a) System
(b) Human participants
(c) Behavior
(d) Artificial environment

_____ 2 The first step in model construction is ________
(a) specify the model.
(b) specify the range of solution values.
(c) observe the system.
(d) none of the above.

_____ 3 The importance of computer simulation is manifested most clearly ____ ___
(a) when one is missing some observations.
(b) if there is a lack of historical data.
(c) if the problem is unique.
(d) the closer the approximation of a model is to reality.

_____ 4 Which of the following approaches involves the attainment of repeated solutions to a problem in order to obtain a distribution of the outcomes?
(a) Chance-constraint programming
(b) Uncertainty transformation
(c) Stochastic linear programming
(d) Linear programming under uncertainty

_____ 5 To receive the greatest benefit from sensitivity analysis, one must be thoroughly familiar with ________
(a) the model.
(b) the strategic variables of the model.
(c) the underlying distributions of the variables.
(d) all the above.

19 Mergers, Acquisitions, and Conglomerate Diversification

Theme Chapter 19 discusses business combinations, provides a rationale for their popularity, and outlines a few models. In addition, historical and empirical information is provided in order to place the activity in this area within the proper perspective.

I The merger movement has been marked by three important and discontinuous periods of activity:

A The first stage in the merger movement, 1885 to 1903, is usually divided into two substages: 1885 to 1893 and 1897 to 1903.

1 With the formation of the Standard Oil Trust in 1885, public and legislative attentions were attracted to mergers. The Sherman Antitrust Act in 1890 was a reflection of this concern.

2 The second substage, which began with prosperity and ended with the 1903 depression, was characterized by the use of holding companies for horizontal mergers in mining and manufacturing.

B The second stage, 1919 to 1929, was distinguished by intense merger activity, primarily in mining, manufacturing, and public utilities.

C The third stage in the merger movement, 1945 to the present, has been aided strongly by the pressures of post-World War II pent-up demands, the rapid rise in prices and profits, and the population boom.

II The two basic procedures for a business combination are

A The merging process invariably begins with some form of negotiations between the managements of the companies.

1 When some agreement on the terms of the acquisition is reached, the board of directors of the two firms are called to ratify the agreement.

2 If ratified, the agreement is submitted to the common stockholders of both companies for approval by an established majority, which is usually two-thirds of the total shares outstanding.

3 If the stockholders approve and the necessary documents have been filed with the states of incorporation, then the merger can be temporarily effected.

(a) The merger may be blocked by the Antitrust Division of the Department of Justice or by the Federal Trade Commision.

(b) However, unless the government can clearly prove that the merger would substantially lessen competition, the merger becomes operational.

B On the other hand, if the management of the merger candidate is recalcitrant, the company which is interested in acquiring it may make a direct appeal to the stockholders through a tender offer.

1 A tender offer is a promise to purchase shares of another corporation, at a specified price usually above the prevailing market price, from any stockholder who wants to tender his shares.
2 Its attractive capital gain has made the tender offer a powerful procedure for company acquisitions.
3 However, the management of the merger candidate may avoid a takeover bid by advising their stockholders to reject the tender offer and/or by merging with another firm.

III The rationale for a business combination is discussed below.

A A firm has two options for survival and growth: internal and external.

1 Internal growth is the growth of a firm along its original or closely related lines of business through the acquisition of assets.
2 External growth is the growth of a firm via the acquisition of other companies and the formation of conglomerate mergers.

B Since the objective of company acquisitions is the long-run maximization of the firm's market value, the acquisition of a company is formally equivalent to the acquisition of an asset.

C There are two general reasons for a business combination: financial considerations and operational considerations.

1 Some financial reasons are
   (a) To reduce the risk of an investment opportunity.
   (b) To employ idle capacity.
   (c) To secure and take advantage of a tax loss.
   (d) To effect more rapid growth through an improvement in profit levels.
   (e) To secure a new source of funds and provide a larger distribution of the company's securities.
   (f) To diversify its activities and sources of revenue.
2 Some operational reasons are
   (a) To improve on the current sales volume and to dampen seasonal and cyclical fluctuations.
   (b) To reduce a dependence on a single product line by providing additional lines of products or services.
   (c) To obtain business in a new territory.
   (d) To obscure from competition the firm's primary area of activity.
   (e) To take advantage of an existing reputation.
   (f) To obtain more competent personnel or technological expertise.
   (g) To acquire patent rights.
   (h) To increase the profitable utilization of present resources.

D Additionally, some personal motivations may also concern a business combination.

1 A merger may enhance the power and prestige of management.
2 It may provide a release for frustrated interests or excess managerial capacity.

E Three reasons are generally offered for the success and popularity of conglomerate mergers:

1 Once an aggressive firm has reached its practical size limit, antitrust policy is effectively applied against horizontal and vertical mergers.
   (a) Hence, a conglomerate merger may be the only means for external growth.
   (b) In addition, the diversification inherent in a conglomerate merger reduces the overall vulnerability of the firm to external influences.

2 Conglomerate mergers are well suited to a fast-growing economy and the concomitant scarcity of financial resources.
3 There is a belief that a synergistic effect accrues to merging firms; i.e., the end result is larger than the sum of the individual parts.
(a) Given the vogue for conglomerate mergers, these companies have managed to attain high price-earnings, *P/E*, multiples.
(b) Furthermore, these companies have an improved ability to attract more capital and to acquire other companies.

IV Exchange ratios in business combinations.

A An exchange ratio is the relative valuation of one good vis-a-vis another good.

B The book value per share can be used as a guide for merger decisions.

1 If the market value per share of a company is considerably below its book value and working capital per share, it is an attractive merger candidate for a liquidity-hungry firm.
2 Such a transaction may become disfunctional in the long run if the acquiring firm cannot improve the earnings of the acquired company.
3 The exchange ratio for book values is defined as

Book value per share of acquiring firm/book value per share of acquired firm

C The market value per share can be used as a guide for merger decisions.

1 Because it portrays the judgment of investors, the market value per share is a more reliable measure of a company's worth than book value.
2 The exchange ratio for market prices is defined as

(Market price per share of acquiring firm x number of shares offered)/market price per share of acquired company

D The acquisition of a firm and the dilution of earnings per share (EPS) in exchange for an increased *P/E* multiple is called the EPS effect.

1 The exchange ratios in a merger determine whether the EPS effect will occur.
2 If it does occur, the soundness of the original merger investment, the market's reaction, and the opportunities available to the new firm will determine whether the new firm can sustain this higher *P/E* multiple.

V Mergers and the level of economic activity.

A Nelson found that peaks in the expansion of business combinations coincided in time with peaks in industrial stock prices, stock market trading, and the establishment of new business ventures.

1 Furthermore, he concluded that high merger activity led peaks in industrial production by a substantial interval.
2 Thus, during the time period of his study, 1895 to 1956, financial reasons were more closely associated with intense merger activity than operating reasons.

B Evidence suggests that average *P/E* ratios can be viewed as a summary measure of the merger climate.

C Griswold's study tends to support the belief that most mergers are initiated by large corporations when the advantage lies with them.

VI Some simple models for merger negotiations and decisions are presented below.

A Stage one: Five steps have been suggested in the search for merger-candidates.

1 Establish a formal group within the organization to coordinate growth and diversification activities.

2 Draw a specific, yet flexible, plan for diversification.
3 Spell out the specific objective to be achieved.
4 Ensure that the company's acquisition policies are clear and sensible.
5 Ensure that all established procedures are compatible with the overall acquisition program of the firm.

B Stage two: Professor Boulden has proposed a model for merger negotiations based on two basic environmental substructures.

1 The emotional environment revolves about the concept of morality and the attendant conflicts.
2 The economic environment revolves about models of the buyer and the seller.
(a) The buyer or acquiring firm attempts to maximize its market value through a sequence of optimizing decisions. The buyer's model assumes the existence of synergistic effects and points out the importance of the market value and P/E ratio of the acquiring firm.
(b) The seller's model is primarily concerned with the form of transaction, legal barriers, and the ability of the market to absorb, at sustained prices, the increased stock outstanding.

C Stage three: Crane's decision model for choosing the best merger candidate from among the preselected set involves three specific steps:

1 Review the firm's objectives and rank them in order of perceived importance.
2 Establish an acceptable procedure for weighting the objectives such that the original rankings are maintained.
3 Match the merger candidates against the ranked and weighted objectives. (Select the candidate with the largest expected value.)

D The model can be further modified by the application of sensitivity analysis to the weights of the objectives or by accounting for the probability of finalizing the prospective acquisition.

1 At this stage, one must consider and evaluate the probability of occurrence of the following factors:
(a) The attitude of the merger candidate's top management toward the merger.
(b) The financial position of the candidate and the ability of its management to thwart a take-over attempt.
(c) The potential competition by other firms that are interested in the same candidate.
(d) The financial and other limitations of the acquiring firm.
2 Thus, a final expected value can be derived for management to consider in making its final decision.

VII A few additional merger considerations warrant mentioning.

A It is difficult to estimate the future cash flows and the expected synergistic effects of an acquisition.

B The financial risk of the acquiring company is likely to be affected by the merging of the two capital structures.

C The business and financial risk of the surviving company will affect the composition and profitability of the firm's entire portfolio of assets.

VIII Risk and diversification in business combinations: a portfolio-selection approach.

A A few assumptions are necessary to transform the acquisition decision into a portfolio selection problem:

1 The management of the acquiring firm possesses a concave downward and quadratic utility function.

2 Management is faced with a list of n acquisition opportunities that are characterized by specific returns and viewed as random variables.
3 The returns of the existing assets are also random variables.
4 The firms involved contain no debt. This assumption eliminates the financial risk component and enables one to concentrate on the diversification of business risk.

B The expected net present value of a project, y, is defined as

$$\text{NPV}_y = \sum_{n=0}^{\infty} \left[\frac{\text{NCF}_n}{(1+r)^n} \right]$$

where n = number of periods in which cash flows are expected
NCF_n = expected net cash flow during nth period
r = risk-free rate of discount

C The variance of the net present value for individual or independent projects is defined as

$$\sigma^2 = \sum_{z=1}^{k} (\text{NPV}_z - \text{NPV}_y)^2 \, P_z$$

where NPV_z = net present value of a series of net cash flows over entire horizon
P_z = probability of occurrence of series

D However, one needs a framework that accounts for the interdependence of cash flows from all investment opportunities. Hence,

$$V_c = \sum_{i=1}^{m} \sum_{j=1}^{m} \text{NPV}_i \, \text{NPV}_j \, \sigma_{ij}$$

where V_c = variance of combination
NPV_i, NPV_j = expected net present values of projects i and j, respectively

If $i = j$, then σ_{ij} is the variance described above, and if $i \neq j$, then σ_{ij} is the covariance between the expected net present values of projects i and j.

E The firm's objective in a merger move is to obtain the best combination of expected net present value and variance. The final solution derives from the portfolio-selection techniques outlined in Chapter 17.

IX Some empirical evidence on conglomerate diversification is presented below.

A The most prominent hypotheses that have been offered to explain merger growth revolve about profitability, synergism, and diversification.

1 Profitability considerations suggest that a firm should pursue investments in any market sector as long as, for any given risk class, the expected rate of return exceeds its cost of capital.
2 Synergism suggests that a firm should grow by a series of capital-deepening (cost-reducing) and capital-widening (output-increasing) investments.
3 Diversification suggests a reduction in the overall level of business risk.

B Smith and Schreiner conducted a study in which portfolio techniques were applied to measure the diversification effectiveness of some conglomerate mergers.

1 They began their work by positing three possible shortcomings from the use of the portfolio approach:
(a) Although conglomerate investment involves both capital and management resources, portfolio selection accounts only for the capital investment.
(b) Although the portfolio investor can vary the extent of his investment or enter into disinvestment, these activities are difficult for a conglomerate.
(c) There is a lack of investment homogeneity in conglomerate acquisitions.
2 The authors derived the following three conclusions:

(a) Overall conglomerate diversification has been less successful and occurred at higher levels of risk than mutual fund diversification.
(b) Certain conglomerates have managed to be close to the best diversifier among mutual funds in that they come closest to the optimal portfolio.
(c) The size and age of the 19 conglomerates in their study did not indicate any substantial correlation with diversification performance.

3 Implied in their study is the fact that the techniques of portfolio selection can be used to construct a portfolio of firms.

QUESTIONS FOR SELF-EXAMINATION

True or False

_____ 1 The merger procedure invariably begins with a tender offer.

_____ 2 The concern over the increased activity in and the influence of mergers precipitated such legislation as the Sherman Antitrust Act.

_____ 3 A merger can be blocked by the government if it would substantially lessen competition.

_____ 4 The two general reasons for a business combination are financial considerations and power.

_____ 5 The application of portfolio-selection techniques to conglomerate investment accounts for the investments in capital and management resources.

_____ 6 The firm's objective in a merger is to obtain the best combination of earnings per share and its P/E multiple.

_____ 7 The final step in choosing the best merger candidate is to match the candidates against the ranked and weighted objectives of management.

_____ 8 An exchange ratio is the relative valuation of one good vis-a-vis another good.

_____ 9 Evidence suggests that average P/E ratios can be viewed as a summary measure of the merger climate.

_____ 10 In light of the shortcomings posited by Smith and Schreiner, portfolio-selection techniques should not be applied to the analysis of business combinations.

Multiple Choice

_____ 1 Which of the following is not a financial or an operational reason for a business combination?
(a) To diversify
(b) To enhance management's prestige
(c) To obtain more competent personnel
(d) To effect more rapid growth

_____ 2 Which of the following is not one of the three reasons generally offered for the success and popularity of conglomerate mergers?
(a) Conglomerate mergers are well suited to a fast growing economy.
(b) Synergistic effects are believed to accrue to merging firms.
(c) Conglomerate mergers are in vogue.
(d) A conglomerate merger may be the only means for external growth.

_____ 3 The acquisition of a firm and the dilution of earnings per share in exchange for an increased P/E multiple is called _____
(a) synergism.
(b) the EPS effect.
(c) the P/E effect.
(d) the liquidity effect.

_____ 4 Which of the following is not one of the steps in Crane's decision model for choosing the best merger candidate?

(a) Establish an acceptable procedure for weighting objectives.
(b) Match the candidates against the objectives.
(c) Review and rank the firm's objectives.
(d) Draw a plan for diversification.

_____ _____ 5 Boulden's model for merger negotiations is based on which two of the following considerations?

(a) The economic environment
(b) The emotional environment
(c) The bargaining strength of the firms
(d) The perceived advantages to each firm

PROBLEMS FOR PRACTICE

1 Firm B is negotiating a merger through an exchange of common stock with Firm A. Firm B will be the surviving company. The following information is available for both firms prior to the merger:

	Firm A	*Firm B*
Capital stock (book value)	$ 875,000	$1,500,000
Retained earnings (book value)	$1,000,000	$3,000,000
Earnings	$ 343,750	$ 750,000
Number of shares	125,000	300,000
Price/earnings ratio	12	22

(a) How many shares of B common stock will be exchanged per share of A common stock based on a 1.0 book value exchange ratio? Determine the number of shares outstanding after the merger. (b) Compute the earnings per share of each firm prior to the merger and the earnings per share of the surviving company, B′. If the P/E ratio of B remains at 22, what is the resultant market price per share of B′?

Solution

(a) Book value of A = ($875,000 + $1,000,000)/125,000 shares
= $15/share

Book value of B = ($1,500,000 + $3,000,000)/300,000 shares
= $15/share

$$\frac{\$15}{\$15} = 1.0 \text{ share of B per share of A}$$

Shares of B′ = 300,000 + (1.0 × 125,000) = 425,000 shares

(b) Before merger:

A EPS = $343,750/125,000 shares = $2.75

B EPS = $750,000/300,000 shares = $2.50

After merger, B′:

Total earnings = $343,750 + $750,000 = $1,093,750

EPS = $1,093,750/425,000 shares = $2.57

Market price = $2.57 × 22 = $56.54

2 For the merger of the two firms, A and B, of Problem 1, the exchange will be based on market values rather than book values. (a) How many shares of B common stock will be exchanged per

share of A common stock based on a 1.0 market value exchange ratio? (b) Determine the earnings per share after the merger of the surviving company, B′. What is the market price per share of B′ if the *P/E* ratio remains at 22? (c) To what level may the *P/E* ratio for B′ decline before the former stockholders of B suffer a decrease in their market value?

Solution

(a) Market value of A = \$2.75 × 12 = \$33/share

Market value of B = \$2.50 × 22 = \$55/share

$\frac{\$33}{\$55}$ = .60 shares of B per share of A

(b) Shares of B′ = 300,000 + (.60 × 125,000) = 375,000 shares

EPS of B′ = \$1,093,750/375,000 shares = \$2.92

Market price of B′ = \$2.92 × 22 = \$64.24

(c) $\frac{\$55}{\$2.92}$ = 18.84 minimum *P/E* to maintain market value of stockholders of B

3 To entice the stockholders of A to exchange their shares for shares of B (from Problem 2), Firm B has offered an additional 25% of their shares than that based on a 1.0 market value exchange ratio. (a) Compute the number of shares of B offered per share of A. How many shares of B′ are outstanding after the merger? (b) Determine the earnings per share of B′ after the merger. If the *P/E* ratio is 22, what is the market price per share of B′? (c) Based on this new exchange ratio, what is the minimum *P/E* ratio for B′ that will maintain the market value of the former stockholders of B?

Solution

(a) .60 + (.25 × .60) = .75 shares of B per share of A

Shares of B′ = 300,000 + (.75 × 125,000) = 393,750 shares

(b) EPS of B′ = \$1,093,750/393,750 shares = \$2.78

Market price of B′ = \$2.78 × 22 = \$61.16

(c) $\frac{\$55}{\$2.78}$ = 19.78 minimum *P/E* to maintain market value of stockholders of B

4 During the merger negotiations between Firm A and B of Problem 1, the stockholders of Firm A argued that the exchange of shares should be based on the contribution of each firm toward the total earnings of the combined company. Determine the ratio of shares exchanged if total earnings were the deciding criterion.

Solution

$\frac{\$343{,}750}{\$750{,}000}$ = .458 ratio of A's earnings to B's earnings

.458 × 300,000 shares = 137,400 shares of B for A's shares

$\frac{137{,}400}{125{,}000}$ = 1.10 shares of B per share of A

PROBLEMS FOR SELF-EXAMINATION

5 Two firms, C and D, have the following financial data:

	Firm C	*Firm D*
Number of shares	60,000	90,000
Earnings per share	\$1.20	\$3.75
Price/earnings ratio	10	16

Firm D is acquiring Firm C through an exchange of common stock. (a) Assuming the exchange is based on a 1.0 market value exchange ratio, determine the number of shares of D required per share of C. Compute the number of shares outstanding after the merger. (b) If the P/E ratio declines to 14 after the merger, what is the resultant market price per share of the new company, D′? (c) Determine the necessary P/E ratio for the new firm to maintain the market value for the former stockholders of Firm D.

Solution

(a)

(b)

(c)

6 Assume the exchange of shares between Firms C and D in Problem 5 was based on the contribution of their respective earnings toward the total earnings of the new firm. (a) Determine the ratio of shares exchanged. (b) Compute the earnings per share of the new firm, D′. If the P/E ratio of Firm D remains at 16, what is the market price per share of Firm D′?

Solution

(a)

(b)

APPENDIX

A Terminology for Mergers and Acquisitions

Theme Appendix A briefly discusses the important distinctions among the various forms of business combinations and introduces some related terminology.

QUESTIONS FOR SELF-EXAMINATION

True or False

_____ 1 Acquisitions and consolidations are subsets of the generic term for business combinations — mergers.

_____ 2 A merger is the transfer of the control of business activity from one corporation to another.

_____ 3 Simply stated, a conglomerate merger is a merger between firms with unrelated products or services.

Multiple Choice

_____ 1 Which of the following is not a specific type of merger?
(a) Horizontal merger
(b) Conglomerate merger
(c) Vertical merger
(d) They all are types of mergers.

_____ 2 A purchase or exchange in which the corporate substances of two companies are combined such that the identity of both firms is retained is called _____
(a) a consolidation.
(b) merging.
(c) an acquisition.
(d) pooling.

_____ 3 An exchange in which the substances of two or more corporations are transferred into a newly formed corporation is called _____
(a) a consolidation.
(b) merging.
(c) an acquisition.
(d) none of the above.

_____ 4 A type of transaction for business combinations in which the candidate is acquired substantially by the securities of the acquiring corporation is called _____
(a) a sale.
(b) an exchange.
(c) a purchase.
(d) a vertical merger.

Answers to Questions for Self-Examination

Chapter 1

True or False	1	2	3	4	5
Answers	T	T	T	F	F

Chapter 2

True or False	1	2	3	4	5	6	7	8	9	10	11
Answers	T	F	F	T	F	F	F	T	T	T	F

Multiple Choice	1	2	3	4	5
Answers	c	d	a	d	b

Chapter 3

True or False	1	2	3	4	5	6	7	8	9	10
Answers	F	T	F	F	T	F	T	F	F	T

Multiple Choice	1	2	3	4	5
Answers	d	b	d	d	c

Chapter 4

True or False	1	2	3	4	5	6	7	8	9
Answers	F	T	F	F	T	F	T	T	F

Multiple Choice	1	2	3	4
Answers	d	b	c	c

Chapter 5

True or False	1	2	3	4	5	6	7	8	9	10
Answers	T	T	F	T	F	F	T	F	F	T

Multiple Choice	1	2	3	4	5
Answers	d	c	a	c	d

Chapter 6

True or False	1	2	3	4	5	6	7	8	9	10
Answers	T	F	T	F	F	T	F	T	T	F

Multiple Choice	1	2	3	4	5
Answers	d	b	a	c	b

Chapter 7

True or False	1	2	3	4	5	6	7	8	9	10	11	12
Answers	T	F	T	F	T	T	T	F	F	T	F	T

Multiple Choice	1	2	3	4	5
Answers	b	a	d	b	d

Chapter 8

True or False	1	2	3	4	5	6	7	8	9	10
Answers	F	F	T	F	F	T	F	F	T	T

Multiple Choice	1	2	3	4	5	
Answers	a	b	c	c	a	.20 > .18

Chapter 9

True or False	1	2	3	4	5	6	7	8	9	10
Answers	T	F	F	T	F	T	F	T	F	T

Multiple Choice	1	2	3	4	5
Answers	c	a	a	b	d

Chapter 10

Multiple Choice	1	2	3	4	5	6	7
Answers	d	c	b	c	b	a	a

Appendix A

True or False	1	2	3	4	5
Answers	T	T	F	T	T

Appendix B

True or False	1	2	3	4	5	6	7	
Answers	T	F	T	T	F	T	T	T

Multiple Choice	1	2	3
Answers	d	b	a & c

Chapter 11

True or False	1	2	3	4	5	6	7	8	9	10
Answers	T	T	F	T	T	F	F	T	T	T

Multiple Choice	1	2	3	4	5
Answers	d	b	c	c	b

Chapter 12

True or False	1	2	3	4	5	6	7	8	9	10
Answers	T	T	T	T	F	T	T	F	F	T

Multiple Choice	1	2	3	4	5
Answers	c	a	b	a	d

Chapter 13

True or False	1	2	3	4	5	6	7	8	9	10
Answers	F	T	T	T	F	F	T	F	T	T

Multiple Choice	1	2	3	4
Answers	b	a	d	b

Chapter 14

True or False	1	2	3	4	5	6	7	8	9	10
Answers	T	F	T	T	T	T	F	T	F	F

Multiple Choice	1	2	3	4	5
Answers	d	c	c	b	b

Chapter 15

True or False	1	2	3	4	5	6	7	8	9	10
Answers	T	T	F	F	T	F	T	F	T	T

Multiple Choice	1	2	3	4	5
Answers	a	b	c	d	a

Chapter 16

True or False	1	2	3	4	5	6	7	8	9	10
Answers	F	T	T	F	T	F	T	T	T	T

Multiple Choice	1	2	3	4	5
Answers	b	c	b	a	d

Chapter 17

True or False	1	2	3	4	5	6	7	8	9	10
Answers	T	F	F	T	T	T	F	T	F	T

Multiple Choice	1	2	3	4	5
Answers	d	a	d	c	a

Chapter 18

True or False	1	2	3	4	5
Answers	F	F	T	T	T

Multiple Choice	1	2	3	4	5
Answers	b	c	d	c	d

Chapter 19

True or False	1	2	3	4	5	6	7	8	9	10
Answers	F	T	T	F	F	F	F	T	T	F

Multiple Choice	1	2	3	4	5
Answers	b	c	b	d	a & b

Appendix A

True or False	1	2	3
Answers	F	T	T

Multiple Choice	1	2	3	4
Answers	d	d	a	b

Answers to Problems for Self-Examination

Chapter 2

4 Project C: Total paid back by fourth year = \$36,000

\$40,000 − \$36,000 = \$4,000 \$4,000/\$12,000 = .33 years

Payback period = 4.33 years

Project D: Total paid back by third year = \$25,000

\$30,000 − \$25,000 = \$5,000 \$5,000/\$10,000 = .5 years

Payback period = 3.5 years

5 Project C: $\sum_{t=1}^{5} B_t = \$48{,}000$ Ratio $= \frac{\$48{,}000}{\$40{,}000} = 1.20$

Project D: $\sum_{t=1}^{5} B_t = \$40{,}000$ Ratio $= \frac{\$40{,}000}{\$30{,}000} = 1.33$

6 Project E: Total paid back by the third year = \$55,000

\$75,000 − \$55,000 = \$20,000 \$20,000/\$30,000 = .67 years

Payback period = 3.67 years

Project F: Total paid back by the third year = \$90,000

Payback period = 3.00 years

7 Project E: $\sum_{t=1}^{6} B_t = \$145{,}000$ Ratio $= \frac{\$145{,}000}{\$\ 75{,}000} = 1.93$

Project F: $\sum_{t=1}^{6} B_t = \$150{,}000$ Ratio $= \frac{\$150{,}000}{\$\ 90{,}000} = 1.67$

Chapter 3

3 Sum of the years = 15

Year	*Cash Flow Before Taxes*	*Cash Flow After Taxes*	*Fraction*	*Depre-ciation*	*Gross Cash Flow*
1	\$20,000	\$10,000	5/15	\$20,000	\$ 30,000
2	20,000	10,000	4/15	16,000	26,000
3	20,000	10,000	3/15	12,000	22,000
4	20,000	10,000	2/15	8,000	18,000
5	20,000	10,000	1/15	4,000	14,000
				\$60,000	\$110,000

4 **Pauly & Sons, sources and uses of funds (1973–1974)**

Sources of Funds	
Decrease in cash	$ 3
Decrease in accounts receivable	1
Decrease in net plant and equipment	5
Increase in bank loan	2
Total sources	$11
Uses of Funds	
Increase in inventories	$ 2
Decrease in accounts payable	4
Decrease in common stock	5
Total uses	$11

5

Year	Cash Flow Before Taxes	Cash Flow After Taxes	Depreciation St. Line	Depreciation D. Bal.	Gross Cash Flow St. Line	Gross Cash Flow D. Bal.
1	$18,000	$9,000	$ 8,000	$16,000	$17,000	$25,000
2	16,000	8,000	8,000	10,667	16,000	18,667
3	14,000	7,000	8,000	7,110	15,000	14,110
4	12,000	6,000	8,000	4,741	14,000	10,741
5	12,000	6,000	8,000	4,741	14,000	10,741
6	12,000	6,000	8,000	4,741	14,000	10,741
			$48,000	$48,000	$90,000	$90,000

6 (a) Straight line:

$$\frac{\$120{,}000}{10 \text{ years}} = \$12{,}000$$

(b) Sum-of-the-years' digits:

$$\text{sum} = 1 + 2 + \cdots + 10 = 55$$

$$\frac{8}{55} \times \$120{,}000 = \$17{,}455$$

(c) Double-declining balance:

$$D_i = \frac{2}{N} C\left(1 - \frac{2}{N}\right)^{i-1}$$

$$D_i = \frac{2}{10}(120{,}000)\left(1 - \frac{2}{10}\right)^{3-1} = \$15{,}360$$

Chapter 4

6

Year	Discount Factor	Cash Flow	Discounted Cash Flow
1	.893	$1,000	$ 893
2	.797	1,500	1,196
3	.712	2,000	1,424
4	.636	2,500	1,590
5	.567	3,000	1,701
			$6,804 PV of cash flows

7 (a) 8% discount rate:

$5,000 × .630 = $3,150 PV of cash flow

$6,000 × .540 = $3,240 PV of cash flow

The *$6,000* payment is preferred since it yields the *highest* PV.

(b) 12% discount rate:

$5,000 × .507 = $2,535 PV of cash flow

$6,000 × .404 = $2,424 PV of cash flow

The *$5,000* payment is now preferred since it yields the *highest* PV.

8

Year	*Discount Factor*	*Cash Flow*	*Discounted Cash Flow*
1	.877	$20,000	$17,540
2	.769	15,000	11,535
3	.675	10,000	6,750
4	.592	5,000	2,960
			$38,785 PV of cash flows

NPV = $38,785 − $42,000 = $−3,215

$$\text{Gross BCR} = \frac{\$38{,}785}{\$42{,}000} = .923$$

Net BCR = .923 − 1.000 = −.077

NPV < 0, gross BCR < 1.0, and net BCR < 0. This investment proposal should be *rejected* using any of the three criteria.

9

Year	*Cash Flow*	*Discount Factor* 10%	8%	*Discounted Cash Flow* 10%	8%
1	$20,000	.909	.926	$18,180	$18,520
2	15,000	.826	.857	12,390	12,855
3	10,000	.751	.794	7,510	7,940
4	5,000	.683	.735	3,415	3,675
				$41,495	$42,990
		PV of cash outflow =		−42,000	−42,000
				$ −505	$ 990

IRR (approximate):

$$8.0\% + \frac{990}{505 + 990}(2.0\%) = 8.0 + 1.32 = 9.32\%$$

Since 9.32% < 14% (cost of capital), *reject* the proposal.

10 (1) 10-year series of interest payments at coupon rate of 8%:

$1,000 × .08 = $80 of interest annually

PV_1 = $80 × 7.360 = $589

(2) Redemption value:

PV_2 = $1,000 × .558 = $558

PV of bond = $589 + $558 = $1,147

11 The maximum amount we should pay is the PV of the cash flows discounted at 12%.

Year	*Discount Factor*	*Cash Flow*	*Discounted Cash Flow*
1	.893	$25,000	$ 22,325
2	.797	40,000	31,880
3	.712	45,000	32,040
4	.636	40,000	25,440
5	.567	25,000	14,175
	Maximum amount =		$125,860 PV of cash flows

12 Project 1:

$\$15,000 \times 2.487 = \$37,305$

$\text{NPV} = \$37,305 - \$20,000 = \$17,305$

$$\text{BCR} = \frac{\$37,305}{\$20,000} = 1.865$$

Project 2:

$\$60,000 \times 2.487 = \$149,220$

$\text{NPV} = \$149,220 - \$120,000 = \$29,220$

$$\text{BCR} = \frac{\$149,220}{\$120,000} = 1.244$$

Ranking:

NPV	*BCR*
Project 2	Project 1
Project 1	Project 2

13 Project A:

Year	*Cash Flow*	*Discount Factor* 10%	*Discounted Cash Flow* 10%
1	$10,000	.909	$ 9,090
2	8,000	.826	6,608
3	6,000	.751	4,506
			$20,204
			−18,000
		NPV =	$ 2,204

Year	*Cash Flow*	*Discount Factor* 16%	*Discount Factor* 18%	*Discounted Cash Flow* 16%	*Discounted Cash Flow* 18%
1	$10,000	.862	.847	$ 8,620	$ 8,470
2	8,000	.743	.718	5,944	5,744
3	6,000	.641	.609	3,846	3,654
				$18,410	$17,868
				−18,000	−18,000
				$ 410	$ −132

IRR (approximate):

$$16.0\% + \frac{410}{410 + 132}(2.0\%) = 16.0 + 1.51 = 17.51\%$$

Project B:

Year	*Cash Flow*	*Discount Factor 10%*	*Discounted Cash Flow 10%*
1	$ 2,000	.909	$ 1,818
2	5,000	.826	4,130
3	5,000	.751	3,755
4	8,000	.683	5,464
5	10,000	.621	6,210
			$21,377
			−18,000
		NPV =	$ 3,377

Year	*Cash Flow*	*Discount Factor 14%*	*Discount Factor 16%*	*Discounted Cash Flow 14%*	*Discounted Cash Flow 16%*
1	$ 2,000	.877	.862	$ 1,754	$ 1,724
2	5,000	.769	.743	3,845	3,715
3	5,000	.675	.641	3,375	3,205
4	8,000	.592	.552	4,736	4,416
5	10,000	.518	.476	5,190	4,760
				$18,900	$17,820
				−18,000	−18,000
				$ 900	$ −180

IRR (approximate):

$$14.0\% + \frac{900}{900 + 180}(2.0\%) = 14.0 + 1.67 = 15.67\%$$

Ranking:

NPV	*IRR*
Project B	Project A
Project A	Project B

Chapter 5

5 Investment C:

$$E(R) = -15(.05) + (0)(.50) + 15(.35) + 30(.10)$$
$$= -.75 + 0 + 5.25 + 3.0 = 7.5\%$$

Investment D:

$$E(R) = 0(.05) + 5(.50) + 10(.35) + 15(.10)$$
$$= 0 + 2.5 + 3.5 + 1.5 = 7.5\%$$

The two opportunities have equal expected returns, thus an investor is indifferent between them.

6 Alternative 1:

$$\$15{,}000 \times 3.312 = \$49{,}680 \quad -40{,}000 \quad NPV = \$\ 9{,}680$$

$$BCR = \frac{\$49{,}680}{\$40{,}000} = 1.242$$

18% Discount Rate

$$\$15{,}000 \times 2.690 = \$40{,}350 \quad -40{,}000 \quad \$\ 350$$

20% Discount Rate

$$\$15{,}000 \times 2.589 = \$38{,}835 \quad -40{,}000 \quad \$-1{,}165$$

IRR (approximate):

$$18.0\% + \frac{350}{350 + 1{,}165}(2.0\%) = 18.0 + .46 = 18.46\%$$

Alternative 2:

$$\$23{,}000 \times (3.993 - .926) = \$70{,}541 \quad -60{,}000 \quad NPV = \$10{,}541$$

$$BCR = \frac{\$70{,}541}{\$60{,}000} = 1.176$$

12% Discount Rate

$$\$23{,}000 \times (3.605 - .893) = \$62{,}376 \quad -60{,}000 \quad \$\ 2{,}376$$

14% Discount Rate

$$\$23{,}000 \times (3.433 - .877) = \$59{,}018 \quad -60{,}000 \quad \$\ -982$$

IRR (approximate):

$$12.0\% + \frac{2{,}376}{2{,}376 + 982}(2.0\%) = 12.0 + 1.42 = 13.42\%$$

Recommendation:

NPV — Alternative 2
BCR — Alternative 1
IRR — Alternative 1

7 Project E:

Cash Flow		*PV Cash Flow*	*Cost*		*Probability*	*E(NPV$_i$)*
$30,000 × 2.487	=	$ 74,610	− $85,000 =	$−10,390 ×	.20	= $−2,078
25,000 × 3.170	=	79,250	− 85,000 =	− 5,750 ×	.30	= −1,725
30,000 × 3.170	=	95,100	− 85,000 =	10,100 ×	.40	= 4,040
35,000 × 3.170	=	110,950	− 85,000 =	25,950 ×	.10	= 2,595
					E(NPV)	= $ 2,832

Project F:

Cash Flow		*PV Cash Flow*	*Cost*		*Probability*	*E(NPV$_i$)*
$32,000 × 3.170	=	$101,440	− $125,000 =	$−23,560 ×	.10	= $−2,356
30,000 × 3.791	=	113,730	− 125,000 =	−11,270 ×	.40	= −4,508
35,000 × 3.791	=	132,685	− 125,000 =	7,685 ×	.30	= 2,306
40,000 × 3.791	=	151,640	− 125,000 =	26,640 ×	.20	= 5,328
					E(NPV)	= $ 770

Project E should be selected since it generates the highest expected net present value.

8

Project E	Project F
2.94% × .2 = 0.588	0.96% × .1 = 0.096
6.85% × .3 = 2.055	6.41% × .4 = 2.564
15.39% × .4 = 6.156	12.40% × .3 = 3.720
23.44% × .1 = 2.344	18.03% × .2 = 3.606
E(IRR) = 11.143%	E(IRR) = 9.986%

Project E remains the preferred project since it has the largest E(IRR) and it is greater than the cost of capital.

9 $\frac{14.5\% - 9.0\%}{(.8 - .4)/.01} = \frac{5.5}{4} = 1.375\%$ return per .01 unit of risk

$9.0\% - \frac{.04}{.01} \times 1.375\% = 9.0 - 5.5 = 3.5\%$ return at zero risk

Since 3.0% < 3.5%, Jim will not enter into the investment.

Chapter 7

6 PV of inflow = $1,125

4% Rate of Return	6% Rate of Return
$ 70 × 11.118 = $ 778.26	$ 70 × 9.712 = $ 679.84
1,000 × .555 = 550.00	1,000 × .417 = 417.00
$1,333.26	$1,096.84

Rate of return (approximate):

$$4.0\% + \frac{1{,}333 - 1{,}125}{1{,}333 - 1{,}097}(2.0\%) = 4.0 + 1.76 = 5.76\%$$

7 PV of inflow = $875

8% Rate of Return	10% Rate of Return
$ 70 × 8.559 = $599.13	$ 70 × 7.606 = $532.42
1,000 × .315 = 315.00	1,000 × .239 = 238.00
$914.13	$771.42

Rate of return (approximate):

$$8.0\% + \frac{914 - 875}{914 - 771}(2.0\%) = 8.0 + .55 = 8.55\%$$

8 Current net earnings = 48,000 shares × $2.00 = $96,000

Current EBIT = $96,000/(1 − T) = $96,000/.6 = $160,000

Incremental EBIT: .15 × $600,000 = $ 90,000
.20 × $600,000 = $120,000

Market price per share = 25 × $2.00 = $50

Additional shares = $600,000/$50 = 12,000 shares

Interest on debt = $600,000 × .09 = $54,000

	Debt Financing (thousands)		Stock Financing (thousands)	
	r = 15%	r = 20%	r = 15%	r = 20%
Current EBIT	$160.0	$160.0	$160.0	$160.0
Incremental EBIT	90.0	120.0	90.0	120.0
Total EBIT	$250.0	$280.0	$250.0	$280.0
Interest	54.0	54.0	—	—
Taxable income	$196.0	$226.0	$250.0	$280.0
Taxes	78.4	90.4	100.0	112.0
Net income	$117.6	$135.6	$150.0	$168.0
EPS	$2.45	$2.83	$2.50	$2.80

If the expansion returns only 15%, stock financing is preferred. Debt financing is preferred if the return is 20%.

Chapter 8

5 Debentures:

$\frac{\$2,500,000}{\$1,000}$ = 2,500 bonds × $920 = $2,300,000 market value

7.5%(1 − T) = 7.5(1 − .4) = 4.5% effective cost

Common stock and retained earnings:

$\frac{\$1.20}{.40}$ = $3.00 EPS × 14 = $42 market value per share

$42 × 100,000 shares = $4,200,000 market value of equity

$K_e = \frac{D}{P} + br = \frac{\$1.20}{\$42} + (.6)(.18) = .137$ = 13.7% effective cost of retained earnings

$K_e = \frac{\$1.20}{\$42(1 - .10)} + (.6)(.18) = .140$ = 14.0% effective cost of new common stock

$3.00 × .6 = $1.80 × 100,000 shares = $180,000 retained earnings available for investment

Market-weighted capital structure:

	Market Values	Market Weights
Debentures	$2,300,000	.354
Equity	4,200,000	.646
	$6,500,000	1.000

.646 × $900,000 = $581,400 equity required

$581,400 − $180,000 = $401,400 new common stock required

$\frac{\$180,000}{\$900,000}$ = .200 market weight for retained earnings

Weighted-average cost of capital:

	Market Weights	Effective Cost (%)	Weighted Cost (%)
Debentures	.354	4.5	1.593
Common stock, new	.446	14.0	6.244
Retained earnings	.200	13.7	2.740
	1.000		10.577%

Chapter 9

4

(Amounts in thousands)	Debt-asset Ratio 0%	10%	20%	30%
Total assets, P_T	\$1,000	\$1,000	\$1,000	\$1,000
Debt, P_d	-0-	100	200	300
Equity, P_e	\$1,000	\$ 900	\$ 800	\$ 700
Net operating income, NOI	\$100	\$100	\$100	\$100
Interest, C_d	-0-	5	10	18
Net income, NI	\$100	\$ 95	\$ 90	\$ 82
Cost-of-equity capital, $K_e = \text{NI}/P_e$	10.00%	10.55%	11.25%	11.71%

Chapter 10, Appendix B

4 Leasing:

$L_t(1 - T) = \$4{,}400(1 - .4) = \$4{,}400 \times .6 = \$2{,}640$

PV of \$1 annually for 6 years at 12% = 4.111

$\text{PV}_L = \$2{,}640 \times 4.111 = \$10{,}853$

Borrow and purchase:

Total cost = \$8,000 × 3 = \$24,000

Salvage value = \$500 × 3 = \$1,500

Depreciation = (\$24,000 − \$1,500)/6 years = \$3,750/year

Down payment = \$24,000(1 − .85) = \$3,600

Amount borrowed = \$24,000 − \$3,600 = \$20,400

PV of \$1 annually for 6 years at 10% = 4.355

Annual loan repayment = \$20,400/4.355 = \$4,684

Interest for first year = \$20,400 × .10 = \$2,040

Year	$B_t + i_t$	i_t	B_t	Unpaid Balance	D_t
1	\$4,684	\$2,040	\$2,644	\$17,756	\$3,750
2	4,684	1,776	2,908	14,848	3,750
3	4,684	1,485	3,199	11,649	3,750
4	4,684	1,165	3,519	8,130	3,750
5	4,684	813	3,871	4,259	3,750
6	4,684	425	4,259	-0-	3,750

Year	$i_t + D_t$	$(i_t + D_t)T$	$B_t + i_t - (i_t + D_t)T$	PV of \$1 at 12%	PV
1	\$5,790	\$2,316	\$2,368	.893	\$ 2,115
2	5,526	2,210	2,474	.797	1,971
3	5,235	2,094	2,590	.712	1,844
4	4,915	1,966	2,718	.636	1,729
5	4,563	1,825	2,859	.567	1,621
6	4,175	1,670	3,014	.507	1,528
					\$10,808

$\text{PV}_B = \$10{,}808 + \$3{,}600 = \$14{,}408$

Since $PV_L < PV_B$, the Wholesale Distributing Company should lease the three trucks.

5 Discounted cost of borrowing-purchase (DCB):

D_t = ($4,000 − $1,000)/2 years = $1,500/year

D_tT = $1,500 × .36 = $540/year

PV of $1 annually for 2 years at 16% = 1.605

PV = $540 × 1.605 = $867

DCB = $4,000 − $867 = $3,133

Discounted cost of leasing (DCL):

Amount of loan = $4,000

Annual payment = $4,000/1.783 = $2,243

Interest, first year = $4,000 × .08 = $320

Principal amount during second year = $4,000 − ($2,243 − $320) = $2,077

Year	L_t	P_t	kP_t	$L_t - kP_t$	$(L_t - kP_t)T$
1	$2,000	$4,000	$320	$1,680	$605
2	2,000	2,077	166	1,834	660

PV: $605 × .862 = $ 522
660 × .743 = 490
$1,012

DCL = $4,000 − $1,012 = $2,988

Since DCL < DCB, Joe should lease the car.

Chapter 11

7 $C^* = \sqrt{\frac{2bT}{i}} = \sqrt{\frac{2 \times \$18 \times \$125{,}000}{(.09 - .04)}} = \sqrt{\frac{4{,}500{,}000}{.05}} = \sqrt{90{,}000{,}000} = \$9{,}487$

8 $\frac{\$4{,}000}{.05}$ = $80,000 net cash released from reduction in float

$80,000 + $40,000 = $120,000 cash released

$21,600,000/360 days = $60,000 daily receipts

$\frac{\$120{,}000}{\$60{,}000}$ = 2 days reduction in float

2 days + 3 days = 5 days float prior to lock-box arrangement

9 Incremental profit: 200 units × ($1,200 − $800) = $80,000

Incremental costs:

Revenue loss from discount offered = 800 units × $1,200 × .02 × .40 = $7,680

Total fixed costs	600 × $200 =	$120,000
Total variable costs	800 × $800 =	640,000
Total costs		$760,000

Total average cost = $760,000/800 units = $950/unit

Current investment in $A/R = \frac{600 \times \$1{,}000}{360/20} = \$33{,}333$

New investment in $A/R = \frac{800 \times \$950}{360/30} = \$63{,}333$

Incremental investment in A/R = \$63,333 − \$33,333 = \$30,000

Increase in bad-debt losses = 800 × \$1,200 × .05 × \$ 950/\$1,200 = \$38,000
600 × \$1,200 × .02 × \$1,000/\$1,200 = 12,000
\$26,000

Total incremental costs = \$7,680 + \$30,000 + \$26,000 = \$63,680

Since the incremental profits > incremental costs, the new credit policy is beneficial.

10 Cost matrix:

Inventory \ Demand	20	30	40	50
20	0	150	300	450
30	200	0	150	300
40	400	200	0	150
50	600	400	200	0

Payoff matrix:

Inventory \ Demand	20	30	40	50	
	Probabilities				*Expected Value*
	.3	.4	.2	.1	
20	1,000	850	700	550	\$ 835
30	800	1,500	1,350	1,200	1,230
40	600	1,300	2,000	1,850	1,285*
50	400	1,100	1,800	2,500	1,170

The recommended level of inventory is 40 snowmobiles since it has the highest expected payoff, as shown by the value with an asterisk.

Chapter 12

6 (a) Firm A:

3/10, net 45 $\frac{3}{97} \times \frac{360}{35} = 31.81\%$

Firm B:

2/20, net 45 $\frac{2}{98} \times \frac{360}{25} = 29.39\%$

The company should pay Firm A and take the discount since its credit terms represent the highest effective annual rate of interest.

(b) Savings from taking cash discount:

.02 × \$10,000 = \$200

Interest cost of bank loan at 12%:

\$9,800 × .12 × (25/360) = \$81.67

Net savings realized:

\$200.00 − \$81.67 = \$118.33

7 $125,000 × .15 = $18,750 compensating balance required

$18,750 − $10,000 = $8,750 additional balance over existing minimum balance

$125,000 × .08 = $10,000 interest cost

$10,000/($125,000 − $8,750) = 8.60% effective rate of interest

8 Average receivables = 30 days × ($300,000/360 days) = $25,000

Amount loaned = $25,000 − $100 = $24,900

Monthly interest = $24,900 × .01 =	$249
Service fee	100
Total monthly charges	$349

$349/$24,900 = 1.402% × 12 months = 16.82% effective annual rate of interest

Chapter 13

4 $P_o = \dfrac{D_o}{k - g}$

$D_o = \$3.23 \times .50 = \$1.62$

g = growth rate: find compound rate such that 2.20 grows to 3.23 in five years

$\dfrac{2.20}{3.23} = .681$ from PV table, g = 8% for .681 in 5-year row

$$P_o = \frac{1.62}{.14 - .08} = \frac{1.62}{.06} = \$27$$

5 $P_c = \dfrac{E}{B_c} + \dfrac{B_a - B_c}{B_c^{\,2}}(E - D)$

$$P_c = \frac{3.00}{.10} + \frac{.06 - .10}{(.10)^2}(3.00 - 1.20)$$

$$= 30.00 + (-7.20) = \$22.80$$

No, the purchase of Box Company's shares for $28 was an unwise decision since the appropriate price per share is only $22.80.

Chapter 15

5 Current ratio = $700,000/$250,000 = 2.8

Quick ratio = ($700,000 − $310,000)/$250,000 = 1.56

Average-collection-period ratio = ($220,000 × 365)/$3,212,000 = 25 days

Receivable-turnover ratio = $3,212,000/$220,000 = 14.6 times

Inventory-turnover ratio = $2,790,000/$310,000 = 9 times

Debt ratio = $800,000/$1,800,000 = 44.44%

Debt-to-equity ratio = $800,000/$1,000,000 = 80.0%

Gross-profit-margin ratio = $422,000/$3,212,000 = 13.14%

Net-profit-margin ratio = $108,000/$3,212,000 = 3.36%

Rate of return on common stock = $108,000/$1,000,000 = 10.8%

Return-on-assets ratio = $108,000/$1,800,000 = 6%

Turnover ratio = $3,212,000/$1,800,000 = 1.78 times

Times-interest-earned ratio = ($180,000 + $40,000)/$40,000 = 5.5 times

6 Net profit margin = earnings after taxes/sales

Earnings after taxes = net profit margin × sales
= .05 × $3,500,000 = $175,000

Return on assets = earnings after taxes/total tangible assets

Total tangible assets = earnings after taxes/return on assets
= $175,000/.08 = $2,187,500

Turnover ratio = sales/total tangible assets
= $3,500,000/$2,187,500 = 1.6 times

7 Debt ratio = total debt/total assets

Total debt = debt ratio × total assets
= .20 × $2,187,500 = $437,500

Net worth = total assets − total debt
= $2,187,500 − $437,500 = $1,750,000

Rate of return on common stock = earnings after taxes/net worth
= $175,000/$1,750,000 = 10%

Chapter 17

3 Total value of final portfolio = $40,000 + $10,000 = $50,000

X_1 = $40,000/$50,000 = .80 proportion for existing portfolio

X_2 = 1.0 − .80 = .20 proportion for additonal security

Portfolio values with the Tacky Gum Company:

$E_p = (.8)(.09) + (.2)(.14) = .100$

$\sigma_p{}^2 = (.8)^2(.06)^2 + (.2)^2(.12)^2 + 2(.8)(.2)(.15)(.12)(.06) = .00323$

$\sigma_p = \sqrt{.00323} = .0568$

Portfolio values with the Loose Glue Company:

$E_p = (.8)(.09) + (.2)(.16) = .104$

$\sigma_p{}^2 = (.8)^2(.06)^2 + (.2)^2(.10)^2 + 2(.8)(.2)(.80)(.06)(.10) = .00424$

$\sigma_p = \sqrt{.00424} = .0651$

The choice between the two companies is not obvious. The decision must be based on Mr. Blunt's unique trade off between risk and return.

Chapter 19

5 (a) Market value of C = $1.20 × 10 = $12

Market value of D = $3.75 × 16 = $60

$12/$60 = .20 shares of D per share of C

Shares of D′ = 90,000 + (.20 × 60,000) = 102,000 shares

(b) Earnings of C = 60,000 shares × $1.20 = $72,000

Earnings of D = 90,000 shares × $3.75 = $337,500

Total earnings of D′ = $72,000 + $337,500 = $409,500

EPS of D′ = $409,500/102,000 shares = $4.01

Market price of D′ = $4.01 × 14 = $56.14

(c) $60/$4.01 = 14.96 minimum *P*/*E* ratio

6 (a) $72,000/$337,500 = .213 ratio of C's earnings to D's earnings

.213 × 90,000 shares = 19,170 shares of D for C's shares

19,170/60,000 = .320 shares of D per share of C

(b) Total shares = 90,000 + 19,170 = 109,170 shares

EPS of D′ = $409,500/109,170 shares = $3.75

Market price of D′ = $3.75 × 16 = $60